The World's Stupidest

POLITICIANS

BARB KARG
AND RICK SUTHERLAND

adamsmedia
avon, massachusetts

Published by
Adams Media, an F+W Publications Company
57 Littlefield Street, Avon, MA 02322. U.S.A.
www.adamsmedia.com

The World's Stupidest Series published by
special arrangement with Michael O'Mara Books Ltd.

ISBN-13: 978-1-59869-573-1
ISBN-10: 1-59869-573-8

Printed in Canada.

J I H G F E D C B A

Library of Congress Cataloging-in-Publication Data
is available from the publisher.

This publication is designed to provide accurate and authoritative
information with regard to the subject matter covered. It is sold
with the understanding that the publisher is not engaged in
rendering legal, accounting, or other professional advice. If legal
advice or other expert assistance is required, the services of a
competent professional person should be sought.

—From a *Declaration of Principles* jointly adopted by a Committee of the
American Bar Association and a Committee of Publishers and Associations

Many of the designations used by manufacturers and sellers
to distinguish their product are claimed as trademarks. Where
those designations appear in this book and Adams Media was
aware of a trademark claim, the designations have been printed
with initial capital letters.

This book is available at quantity discounts for bulk purchases.
For information, please call 1-800-289-0963.

This book is dedicated to long-suffering political constituents the world over: those patient souls who've been forced to endure too many idiotic elected officials whose shenanigans have managed to make the rest of humanity appear utterly noble.

And to all the moronic politicos who made this book possible with their ridiculous rhetoric, incessant lying, adultery, illicit debauchery, criminal acts, verbal carnage, and major hissy fits.

Acknowledgments

Writing and producing a book is never an easy endeavor and *The World's Stupidest Politicians* is no exception to the rule. Thankfully, we're surrounded by a host of exceptional individuals who it is our privilege to know and to work with. For starters, we'd like to thank the fine folks at Adams Media with whom we've had the pleasure of working for many years. We offer our highest regards to director of innovation Paula Munier, the most brilliant gal we know, whose *joie de vivre* we appreciate and who we adore way more than cabernet and chocolate (and *that's* saying something!). We also salute Brendan O'Neill for his constant dedication, tenacity, and above all his sense of humor on each and every project. You guys are the best! As always, we also offer our sincere thanks to copy chief Sheila Zwiebel, director of manufacturing Sue Beale, and proofer Laraine Lach for their tireless and exceptional work. You guys are a fabulous team and we greatly appreciate everything you do.

On the homefront, we forever have the unending support of our families and friends, all of whom we would be lost without and who know that we've never *ever* done anything stupid. Uh huh. Our thanks to Ma, Pop, Dad, Chrissy, Glen, Anne, Terry, Kathy, the Blonde Bombshell, Ellen and Jim, Jeans and Jim, Jim V., Karla, Linda B., the Scribe Tribe, and the two newest additions to our family, Ethan and Brady. You guys have all been a constant support and we consider your love and friendship one of the greatest gifts we could ever hope for. We love you all very much. We'd like to give a special shout to Chrissy Grant, Ellen Weider, and Trudi Karg for their exceptional research, plowing through our endless humorous rantings, and keeping us on the straight and narrow. To Ma, we'd like to offer additional accolades for her patience in helping us pull everything together. And last, but certainly not least, we thank our flurry of four-legged children, Piper, Jazz, Jinks, Maya, and Scout, who bring joy to our every waking moment. And our dear Sasha, Harley, and Mog who are always in our thoughts.

Many thanks to all of you!
Barb and Rick

Introduction

Politician (pall-uh-tish-an)

A civic-minded, kind-hearted soul possessing superior communication skills, compassion, and a drive that compels them to commit to being a public servant in order to help make the world a better place.

Stupid Politician (stoo-pid pall-uh-tish-an)

A devious, narrow-minded schmuck who, once elected, is overcome with the need for power, imbibing, retracting all candidacy promises, hiring strippers, committing adultery, and forgoing the ability to spell or pronounce simple words like "potatoe" and "nuke-you-lure."

When you compare the politicians and orators of ancient Egypt, Rome, and Greece to the gaggle of current world leaders you'll find that nothing has changed. The same ridiculous backstabbing rhetorical nonsense is still being played out in the same basic forum regardless of whether it's the ancient Roman Senate or

Capitol Hill. And the best part is that while a great many of these "noble" politicos have made their marks in history, much of their abominable behavior and underhandedness will tarnish their legacies for generations, and just maybe, serve as examples of how not to turn public service into a public disgrace.

One theory in big business is that people are often promoted to their highest level of incompetence by moving someone who's pretty good at one job into a position of responsibility that they're just barely capable of handling—and they spend a lot of their time covering up their deficiencies. Is this true in politics? We hate to be cynical (yeah, *right*), but the answer is yes, and we think the theory carries a lot more substance. In the world of politics, there is one unflappable truth. Politicians lie. Not just one or two, or even two hundred. All of them—from local yokels to Commanders-in-Chief—bend the truth to suit their needs under the guise of actually helping constituents. What they say and do *before* they're elected and what they say and do *after* they're elected is the difference between a Grade A prime rib and a SPAM meatloaf, and there's just no getting around it. Across the board they *all* suffer from *electile* dysfunction and there's no little blue pill to straighten things out.

In this zippy little tome of political debauchery you'll find a full service of political quotes, bumper stickers, quizzes, awards, and a smorgasbord of dismaying accounts describing deceit, illicit affairs, arrogant lawlessness, and assorted absurd behavior that would make Caligula cringe. No one hopes that politicians will fall on their faces and embarrass their friends, families, and the people who trusted them enough to vote them into office, but it does happen with alarming regularity. And you can bet your voter registration card that when it does, we're all gonna gather 'round the bonfire, break out the skewers, and have ourselves a wienie roast. In this buffet of political buffoonery you'll find:

Stupid Says . . . • Lamebrain political quotes
Bumper Snickers! • Dimwit car decorations
Democratic Dimwits • When donkeys make asses of themselves
Heels on Wheels • Politically incorrect rides

Presidential Pinheads • Executive eggheads

Just Say *Duh*! • Stupid political blunders

Politicos in the Pokey • Political scofflaws

Lost in Translation: • What you say and what a stupid politician hears

The Proverbial Politician • Words lame-brain politicos live by

Nitwits in the News • Halfwit headliners

Democracy Inaction • When the wheels of democracy fall off the cart

Republican Numbnuts • When elephants go on a rampage

Film at Eleven • Favorite flicks of daft politicos

The Peabrain Politico Dictionary • The "moronic politician" meaning of words and phrases

Promises, Promises . . . • What candidates promise but don't deliver

Sex, Lies, and Videotape • Illicit infractions behind closed doors

The Ten Commandments of Stupid Politicians

I. Thou shalt always make certain that if you lie, cheat, or steal, you can beat a polygraph test.

II. Thou shalt only use the phrase "read my lips" for influential CEOs, interns, and busty chicks at $2,000 a plate fundraisers.

III. Thou shalt not worship false deities save for Ralph Nader, Maya Angelou, and, above all, Keith Olbermann.

IV. Thou shalt always take care that when having an affair, you're never late on your blackmail payments.

V. Thou shalt never forget where you've buried the bodies.

VI. Thou shalt always remember if you have to fight—fight dirty.

VII. Thou shalt always maintain there are at least ten bastards in the room who are more evil than you are.

VIII. Thou shalt never under any circumstances give up expensive booze, strippers, bribes, or off-shore bank accounts.

IX. Thou shalt always maintain at any and all costs that your I.Q. is higher than an ice cube.

X. Thou shalt always remember that when facing an indictment, always take everyone else down with you.

Just Say *Duh*!

In yet another prime example of wasted tax-payer dollars, we present to you the shenanigans of right wing religious zealot and former Attorney General John Ashcroft, who in 2002 unleashed his prudish conservatism on a poor defenseless statue. Yes, a statue. The Spirit of Justice to be exact, a piece of art that since the 1930s has stood in the Justice Department's Great Hall. With her arms out-stretched, Lady Justice depicts a woman wearing a toga that covers one breast, leaving the other to become the target of Ashcroft's sexually repressed Republican rage. Her counterpart in the hall is "The Majesty of Law," a partially clad male figure. Press conferences held in the DOJ usually show-cased Lady Justice as a backdrop to the podium, her naked—*gasp*—breast exposed to the minions. Outraged at having to share photo ops with such a salacious wench, Ashcroft whined until a set of drapes—to the tune of $8,000—was purchased to cover her up. For those counting, that eight grand would've fed several thousand starving Ethiopian children for two years.

The Proverbial Politician

A bribe a day keeps the
indictment away.

Bumper Snickers!

MY SON IS WARMONGER OF THE MONTH!
Barbara Bush

LACK OF HEALTHCARE IS MERELY THE SLOW-
EST POSSIBLE RATE AT WHICH ONE CAN DIE.
John Edwards

Democratic Dimwits

Sure signs you're dealing with a dunderheaded
elected Democrat.

They can't complete a sentence without
uttering the phrase "vast right wing
conspiracy."

The closest they've ever come to the rain for-
est is attending a Sting concert.

Film at Eleven

Favorite films of the truly daft.

William Rehnquist: *A Streetcar
Named Retire*

Ralph Nader: *Indiana Jones and
the Last Campaign*

Al Gore: *A View to a Spill*

Democracy Inaction

Suffering from a severe case of the perks, George Bush's White House Chief of Staff John Sununu managed to embarrass the administration in early 1991, because he'd developed the habit of commandeering Air Force jets for missions of great national concern—such as trips to Colorado ski resorts and visits to his Boston dentist. The word came down from the Prez that Sununu was to knock off the free plane rides. But, Bush didn't say anything about *cars*, right? When Sununu was suddenly overcome with the urge to buy a few rare stamps, he had a White House limousine drive him 225 miles from Washington, D.C., to New York's Christie's Auction House. In those days before the proliferation of small cellular telephones, Sununu's reasoning for using taxpayer dollars to go on personal adventures was that he needed to be "on the phone constantly" talking with Congressmen, Senators, and fellow Cabinet members about important issues, and that this is "in the national interest." Somehow we doubt that the Senate, Congress, or the nation found Sununu's side trips even vaguely interesting. Neither did Bush, and Sununu was asked to resign a few months later. Moron.

The Peabrain Politico Dictionary

Limited liability: Short term fibbing

Private sector: What got Monica Lewinsky in hot water

Reaganomics: What Nancy spent on the White House china

Stupid Says . . .

66If I don't have a woman every three days or so I get a terrible headache.99

—John F. Kennedy

Republican Numbnuts

Sure signs you're dealing with a harebrained elected Republican.

Their idea of whooping it up at a party is removing their bow tie.

They think a president lying about his sex life is more serious than a president lying about his reasons for going to war.

Promises, Promises . . .

WHAT THE CANDIDATE PROMISES:
That he'll become intrinsically involved in foreign affairs.

WHAT THE ELECTED OFFICIAL DOES:
Two Swedish mistresses, one Bolivian stripper, and a trio of busty Austrian barmaids.

Sex, Lies, and Videotape

In late 1998, self-righteous outrage over President Bill Clinton's affair with Monica Lewinsky, particularly from the Republican contingent in Congress, took a major hit when House Speaker Bob Livingston admitted that he'd had extra-marital dalliances to Republican colleagues as they prepared to debate the merits of impeaching Clinton. Facing a crush of damning publicity, Livingston bailed out by announcing his resignation as Speaker of the House and would resign his Congressional seat in May of 1999. Livingston attempted to spin his resignation by claiming that he was setting an "example" that he hoped the President would follow. Clinton—ever the consummate politician—countered by saying that he liked and respected Livingston and urged him to stay in office. Livingston wasn't the only Congressman to get burned in the backfiring Clinton witch-hunt. Henry Hyde, chairman of the House Judiciary Committee who was bringing impeachment proceedings against Clinton, was revealed to have strayed. Helen Chenoweth of Idaho confessed to an affair, and Dan Burton of Illinois admitted to an out of wedlock child. Never mind throwing stones. People who live in glass houses should just keep their pants on.

WHAT'S THE DIFFERENCE BETWEEN BILL CLINTON, DAN QUAYLE, AND JANE FONDA?

FONDA WENT TO VIETNAM.

Politicos in the Pokey

Taking a particularly disturbing dip into the dark side of humanity, we present to you Republican activist Parker Bena, a member of the Virginia Electoral College during the 2000 presidential election. In 2001, Bena was convicted of possessing child pornography on his computer, a fact he initially lied about. It's alleged that this moron actually claimed he just casually received "unsolicited" e-mails with explicit pictures of children—some as young as three. Yeah, *right*. Turns out the perv downloaded the images off porn Web sites. Sicko. Bena was sentenced to thirty months in the slammer and ordered to pay $18,000 in fines. Ain't it swell that this poor excuse for humanity helped elect Dubya?

Republican Numbnuts

Sure signs you're dealing with a harebrained elected Republican.

They think NPR is the bullhorn of the devil.

They're terrified of the polar ice caps melting, but wouldn't dream of giving up their air conditioning.

Democratic Dimwits

Sure signs you're dealing with a dunderheaded elected Democrat.

They think Charles Manson can actually be reformed and rejoin society.

They foolishly assume there will be a Social Security payment waiting for them when they retire.

The Frivolous Fancy Pants Award

It's no secret that Washington, D.C., is full of political wacknuts, but administrative law judge Roy Pearson set a new standard in May 2005 when he took the pants from his $1,000 suit to Custom Cleaners, owned by South Korean immigrants Soo and Jin Chung, for alteration. A few days later the trousers mysteriously disappeared. After a week, Soo returned the pants, which Pearson claimed weren't his because they had cuffs and the pattern differed. After his initial monetary demands weren't met, the Pantless Wonder sued the Chungs on grounds that they *and* their "Satisfaction Guaranteed" and "Same Day Service" signs constituted fraud. For two years litigation dragged on, with Pearson—representing himself—starting his suit at $67 million, and later lessening the sum to $54 million. Included in his "damages" was a fee for a rental car which he'd have to use for a decade in order to use another dry cleaner that wasn't within walking distance of his home. In May 2007, the Chungs won the case and Judge Cranky Pants was ordered to pay court costs, but not the Chung's legal bills amounting to $100,000. Can't wait for the appeal . . .

Dumb and Dumberer

During a visit to the U.K., Dubya meets with Queen Elizabeth, and asks her what makes her a successful leader. She replies that she surrounds herself with intelligent people. He asks how she knows if someone is intelligent. "By asking the right questions." She picks up the phone and calls Tony Blair. "Mr. Blair. Your father has a child and your mother has a child, but this child is not your brother or sister. Who is it?" Without hesitation, Blair answers: "Why it's me, Your Highness." The Queen grins. "Correct," she says, turning to Dubya. "Now do you understand?" He nods. "I'll get right on that." Upon returning home, Dubya calls Tom DeLay. "Tom. Your pappy has a kid and your mama has a kid, but they ain't your brother or sister. Who are they?" DeLay is stumped. "I'll get back to you." DeLay then calls an emergency senatorial meeting, but no one knows the answer. Desperate, he phones Hillary Clinton and asks her the question. Clinton laughs. "It's me, of course." DeLay thanks her profusely and immediately calls Dubya. "I have the answer, sir. It's Hillary Clinton!" Dubya snorts. "Wrong, you moron. It's Tony Blair."

The Peabrain Politico Dictionary

Free trade: A night with an intern

Coup d'état: An hors d'oeuvre with caviar

Grassroots democracy: Legalizing
marijuana

Bumper Snickers!

IF AT FIRST YOU DON'T SUCCEED,
DESTROY ALL THE EVIDENCE THAT YOU
TRIED.
Richard Nixon

OUR GOVERNOR IS MORE CROOKED THAN
YOUR GOVERNOR!
Former Illinois governor George Ryan

The Proverbial Politician

Out of hindsight, out of mind.

Nitwits in the News

Remember all those lame excuses you used to use in high school, like "my hamster chewed up my homework" and "I don't know how this switchblade got in my locker?" Well, none of those retorts would work on Alexander Kuzmin. Why, you ask? Because as the mayor of Megion, a city in Western Siberia, Kuzmin has a certain measure of power, one that enables him to issue a ban on excuses. Yes, excuses. Twenty-seven of them to be exact—none of which are allowed to be uttered by civil servants. Banned verbiage includes: "I don't know," "It's not my job," "I'm having lunch," "The working day is over," "I'm not dealing with this," "I think I was sick at the time," and "There's no money." So, if you happen to be vacationing in Megion (and you don't mind possibly ending up in a Siberian gulag), you might find some amusement by dropping into town hall at lunchtime to ask a bunch of really annoying questions.

Promises, Promises . . .

WHAT THE CANDIDATE PROMISES:
That he will close down the borders in an effort to curtail illegal immigration.

WHAT THE ELECTED OFFICIAL DOES:
Hires a household staff of forty, none of whom have green cards.

The Peabrain Politico Dictionary

Neofeudalism: The Matrix trilogy

Kurdification: The nationalization of cottage cheese

Axis of Evil: When Brian Boitano meets Osama Bin Laden

Film at Eleven

Favorite films of the truly daft.

Barack Obama: *Who's Afraid of Hillary Clinton?*

The Bush twins: *Children of a Lesser Clod*

Larry Craig: *All About Steve*

Stupid Says . . .

66 Everyone knows that you're not really a real man unless you own a gun. 99

—Dick Cheney

The Proverbial Politician

The taxman doesn't fall far from the fee.

Nitwits in the News

It's no secret that budget meetings can be stressful and can incite strong debate among politicians, but Iulian Florea crossed the line in September 2007 during a council meeting. Florea is the mayor of Teslui, a town in southwestern Romania. His previous career was as a professional boxer. Not a good combination. When an argument ensued over the Teslui budget, Mayor Florea snapped and attacked councilor Mircea Chirita. The scuffle caused four other council members to come to Chirita's aid. Bad plan. Florea took one of 'em out with an upper cut, another with a left hook, and walloped the other two members, both of whom ended up with concussions. As one might expect, all five of his opponents are now suing him. If there's anything to be gleaned from Florea's little hissy fit it's that we no longer need to guess what would happen if Mike Tyson was elected to office.

Democratic Dimwits

Sure signs you're dealing with a dunderheaded elected Democrat.

They have a special room in their house filled with Hubert Humphrey paraphernalia.

In high school they were voted "Most Likely to Join the Peace Corps."

Stupid Says . . .

66You can tell a lot about a fellow's character by his way of eating jelly beans.99

—Ronald Reagan

The Peabrain Politico Dictionary

Saffronization: Yellow journalism

Monarchy: The study of butterflies

Communism: Living with a bunch of hippies

Just Say *Duh*!

It's not uncommon for politicians to proverbially "shoot themselves in the foot," but Colombian Lord Mayor Rafael Augusto Galan Cuervo took things one step further. In a classic example of why there should be universal gun control, Cuervo, who is the mayor of the northern town of Ramiriqui, was accompanying a group of pilgrims to the local church when he needed to take a pitstop at the little mayor's room. With a pistol in his pocket—literally—Cuervo lowered his trousers to use the facilities and in doing so discharged his weapon. The pistol, that is. The resounding gunshot and subsequent yelling drew attention to the bathroom, where it was discovered that Cuervo had shot himself in the arse. It goes without saying that this particular mayoral incident, dare we say, was a bum deal.

The Proverbial Politician

Crime flies when you've got a gun.

Promises, Promises . . .

WHAT THE CANDIDATE PROMISES:
*A significant tax increase for anyone earning
over a million dollars.*

WHAT THE ELECTED OFFICIAL DOES:
*Mandate a 40 percent tax hike
for middle income households.*

Stupid Says . . .

❝If everybody in this town connected with
politics had to leave town because of chasing
women and drinking, you would have no
government.❞

—Barry Goldwater

Curtain Call

It's after midnight and George Dubya is in the White House kitchen eating pork rinds when he suddenly sees the ghost of George Washington. "Mr. President," says Dubya. "Please tell me what I can do to make America the most powerful nation in the world?" Without hesitation, Washington answers: "You must follow in my footsteps by being unequivocally honest and set an honorable example for everyone." The next night, Dubya is again raiding the White House fridge when he happens upon the ghost of Thomas Jefferson. "Mr. President," says Dubya. "Please tell me what I can do to keep American citizens healthy?" Without hesitation, Jefferson answers: "You must cut taxes and install a national health care plan." On the third night, Dubya gets up to use the little president's room when he runs into the ghost of Abraham Lincoln. "Mr. President," Dubya says. "Please tell me what I can do to make every American happy?" Without hesitation, Lincoln answers: "Go see a play."

The Hypocritical Halfwit of the Millennium Award

Preparing for an ill-conceived 2008 presidential bid, Congressional loudmouth Newt Gingrich publicly confessed to extra-marital affairs in a transparent attempt at pre-emptive damage control, before the media skewered him. If you remember, Gingrich led the effort to impeach Bill Clinton after the Monica Lewinsky affair, but Gingrich made the disingenuous claim that the only reason he'd sought the President's head was because Clinton had lied to Congress. Gingrich has long been a notorious philanderer during his terms in political office, and as Speaker of the House, eighty-four ethics charges were brought against him. For his years of unabashed false virtue and sanctimonious posturing, Gingrich gets our Hypocritical Halfwit of the Millennium Award hands down.

Heels on Wheels

If politicians had cars named after them,
what would they be?

Ann Coulter: Honda Harpy

Gary Hart: Chevy Capricious

Larry Craig: PT Airport Lounge Cruiser

Lost in Translation

WHAT YOU SAY:
You swore you wouldn't raise taxes!

WHAT A STUPID POLITICIAN HEARS:
I'm not poor even after I pay taxes!

Sex, Lies, and Videotape

One of the most absurd examples of ego-maniacal Congressional misdeeds and power abuse came to light when Bob Packwood, a Republican senator from Oregon, was exposed to charges of sexual harassment and assault—and the most damning evidence came from his own diary. First elected in 1968, Packwood had chaired the Senate Finance Committee and was considered an influential moderate voice in the Senate. His political career began skidding in 1992 after a *Washington Post* story revealed charges of sexual abuse by ten former staffers and lobbyists. During a Congressional investigation, Packwood's diary became the center of attention and he was forced to turn over more than 10,000 pages, much of which had clearly been altered to conceal original entries. By the time the Senate Ethics Committee recommended expelling Packwood from the Senate, he'd been accused of sexual misconduct against seventeen women and attempting to use his power to get his wife a job. Packwood dodged the expulsion and resigned on September 7, 1995. Dear diary indeed!

The Proverbial Politician

Too many crooks spoil the sloth.

Politicos in the Pokey

In 2001, El Paso County Republican activist, lawyer, and GOP state official Randal David Ankeney met with a thirteen-year-old girl in Colorado. He plied her with marijuana, took topless pictures of her, and attempted to sexually assault her. After resigning from Colorado Republican Governor Bill Owen's administration, Ankeney was convicted of the offense, and was sentenced to two years in the slammer. Five years later, he was at it again, this time charged with nine felonies for sexual assault and exploitation on a child. At the time that incident took place, Ankeney was out on bond for a different set of charges for sexually assaulting a woman. And this guy was a "rising star in the GOP"? Will someone please lock this dirtbag up for good this time? Sheesh.

Democracy Inaction

The state of Illinois, like a handful of other states, has a reputation for corrupt political practices, not the least of which are a trio of Illinois governors who've been convicted of felony charges. One of the more curious conundrums stemming from Honest Abe's old stomping grounds is the mystery surrounding Illinois Secretary of State Paul Powell, who died in October of 1970. For the record, Powell never made over $30,000 a year during his four decades of public service, but when he passed, his estate was worth over $2 million. Even more mysterious was the fact that a few days after his death, $800,000 of that estate was found in his hotel room jammed into shoeboxes, strongboxes, and briefcases. Say what? For a good ol' country boy with a charming reputation, something just isn't adding up.

Open Mouth. Insert Foot.

Match the pinheaded politico with their bone-headed blather.

a. Richard Nixon

b. Marion Barry

c. Jesse Ventura

d. Al Sharpton

e. Dan Quayle

f. George Wallace

g. Joseph P. Kennedy

1. "Trees cause more pollution than automobiles."

2. "I have no political ambitions for myself or my children."

3. "Segregation now, segregation tomorrow, segregation forever."

4. "You may be sure that the Americans will commit all the stupidities they can think of, plus some that are beyond imagination."

5. "I would have made a good Pope."

6. "We are not ready for an unforeseen event that may or may not occur."

7. "We need an energy bill that encourages consumption."

h. Charles De Gaulle

8. "Outside of the killings, Washington has one of the lowest crime rates in the country."

i. Ronald Reagan

9. "Whoever designed the streets must have been drunk. . . . I think it was those Irish guys."

j. George Dubya Bush

10. "I believe that gays and lesbians deserve to have the same rights as homosexuals."

Answers:
1-i, 2-g, 3-f,
4-h, 5-a, 6-
e, 7-j, 8-b,
9-c, 10-d

Presidential Pinheads

In the annals of presidential history, more than a few Commanders-in-Chief have been personally attacked, whether by members of their opposing party, the media, other world leaders, or even assassins and terrorists, but only one was attacked by a killer bunny. The incident took place in April of 1979, when President Jimmy Carter was vacationing at his farm in Plains, Georgia. According to Carter's press secretary Jody Powell, Carter was fishing on his pond when he spotted a "large animal swimming toward him." Said creature turned out to be a "swamp rabbit," the legendary equivalent of the Anti-Christ Easter Bunny, complete with "gnashing" teeth and splayed paws. Uncertain of the hissing bunny's intent, Carter apparently pushed it aside with an oar. Of course, once the story leaked, it became a media frenzy that would follow the President for years. Had P.E.T.A. been paying attention, Carter would surely have been impeached.

WHERE'S THE BEST PLACE
TO TAKE A PICTURE
OF THE BUSH
ADMINISTRATION?

IN A POLICE
LINE-UP.

The Proverbial Politician

A watched plot is never foiled.

Democratic Dimwits

Sure signs you're dealing with a dunderheaded elected Democrat.

They believe everything they read in the *Washington Post* and *Page Six*.

They insist that greedy oil companies are suppressing the fact that vehicles can actually run on tap water.

Heels on Wheels

If politicians had cars named after them, what would they be?

Karl Rove: Acura Legend in My Own Mind

Bill Clinton: Oval Office Hummer

Lyndon Johnson: Cadillac Escalate

Presidential Pinheads

One of the most important jobs a president has is that of international diplomat, effectively communicating with other world leaders and upper echelon mucky mucks. Some presidents were masters of international relations. Others . . . uh . . . not so much. Case in point George Bush, who in January of 1992 was in Japan engaging in a formal state dinner at the home of Japanese Prime Minister Kiichi Miyazawa. Did he talk about a free trade agreement or a resolution to world hunger? Nope. Instead he barfed all over his big bad self before passing out in the Prime Minister's lap. Citing the intestinal flu as the reason for his Technicolor yawn, Bush eventually arose from his fainting spell and bailed on the dinner. As a nation, we couldn't have been more proud of Bush's explosive foreign trade policy.

Bumper Snickers!

> I CAN GO FROM ZERO TO BITCH IN 1.4 SECONDS.
> Ann Coulter

> A VILLAGE IN TEXAS IS MISSING ITS IDIOT.
> Al Sharpton

Film at Eleven

Favorite films of the truly daft.

Dan Quayle: *Gunga Dingbat*

Rush Limbaugh: *Broadcast Ruse*

Ted Kennedy: *Crouching Tiger, Hidden Flagon*

Presidential Pinheads

William Jefferson Clinton left his mark on the White House in a big . . . uh . . . memorable way. We all know the story. President meets busty brunette intern. Intern becomes obsessed with the Prez. Billy and his little interior secretary invest in a few Cuban cigars. Intern goes all *Fatal Attraction* on the Prez and plays "finders keepers" with a GAP dress, and Billy spends the rest of his years in office arguing the definition of the word "is." And lest we forget, there was an entire gaggle of women in various stages of accusatory rage, including Paula Jones, Gennifer Flowers, Kathleen Willey, and Juanita Broaddrick. It's a wonder Billy Boy got any actual work done. As is typical when scandal is the name of the game, all the good Clinton accomplished will forever be tarnished by a single word: Lewinsky. Let's face it. All we really want to know is what was up with the cigars, and why in Hades didn't Monica take that damn dress to the cleaners?

The Peabrain Politico Dictionary

Speaker of the House: A home
intercom system

Ombudsman: A beer swilling yogi

Magna Carta: What comes out of
Mt. Etna when she blows

The Proverbial Politician

Abstaining makes the vote grow stronger.

Democratic Dimwits

Sure signs you're dealing with a dunderheaded
elected Democrat.

They attend Gay Pride events so as not to be
dubbed homophobic.

They support public education, but send
their kids to private boarding schools in
Switzerland.

WHAT HAPPENS WHEN YOU CROSS A DEMOCRAT WITH A PILGRIM?

YOU GET A **GOD-FEARING** TAX COLLECTOR WHO GIVES THANKS FOR WHAT OTHER PEOPLE **HAVE.**

Nitwits in the News

It was September 2007, when conservative German politician Gabriele Pauli dropped a bombshell on Bavarian citizenry and politicos when she proposed that civil marriages have a time limit. Huh? Pauli, a member of Bavaria's ultra-conservative Christian Social Union (CSU), was running a campaign to become head of her party when she unleashed her seven year itch plan. Civil marriages would be limited to seven years, after which the union would lapse and couples would have to officially renew their vows if they decided to continue their relationship. According to Pauli, this "contract" would ultimately save money and emotional distress as a result of divorce. Serving as district administrator of the county of Fürth, Pauli is no stranger to divorce, having already been hitched and unhitched twice. And then there's that little matter of her posing for a magazine in dominatrix garb and her publicly calling for the resignation of Bavaria's revered minister-president Edmund Stoiber. Running in a predominantly Catholic region, Pauli lost the election by a landslide, an obvious dose of karma for getting German Pope Benedict's knickers in a twist.

The Proverbial Politician

Indiscretion is the better part of valor.

Mix and Mingle: Rabid Republican Anagrams

a. Mitt Romney
b. Bob Packwood
c. Pat Robertson
d. Donald Rumsfeld
e. Arnold Schwarzenegger
f. Condoleezza Rice
g. Alexander Haig
h. Ann Coulter
i. Dick Cheney
j. Larry Craig

1. CHICKEN DYE
2. KABOB COWPAD
3. CRAZE DECOLONIZE
4. RAG LIARCRY
5. UNCLEAN ROT
6. MINTY METRO
7. LANDLORDS FUMED
8. GROWL ENHANCED GRAZERS
9. SNORT PROBATE
10. AGED HERNIALAX

Answers:
1-i, 2-b, 3-f,
4-j, 5-h, 6-
a, 7-d, 8-e,
9-c, 10-g

Film at Eleven

Favorite films of the truly daft.

John F. Kennedy: *All the President's Women*

Trent Lott: *Pain Man*

Jerry Falwell: *The Adventures of Robbing the Hood*

Promises, Promises . . .

WHAT THE CANDIDATE PROMISES:
A national healthcare plan whereby every citizen is granted medical insurance.

WHAT THE ELECTED OFFICIAL DOES:
Cuts Medicare spending by $100 million and allows insurance companies to triple their premiums.

Stupid Says . . .

66Those who survived the San Francisco earthquake said, 'Thank God, I'm still alive.' But, of course, those who died, their lives will never be the same again.99

—Barbara Boxer

Republican Numbnuts

Sure signs you're dealing with a harebrained elected Republican.

They complain about welfare subsidies, but rely on tax breaks and off-shore accounts.

One word: Halliburton.

Promises, Promises . . .

WHAT THE CANDIDATE PROMISES:
To pull all active troops out of war-torn nations.

WHAT THE ELECTED OFFICIAL DOES:
Decides to bomb another country and send more troops.

Politicos in the Pokey

Politicians often become household talking points for all the wrong reasons, and Washington, D.C., Mayor Marion Barry became the poster child for the concept in 1990. Barry was the focus of an elaborate sting operation conducted by the FBI and members of the D.C. police internal affairs department, during which he was videotaped smoking crack cocaine with former girlfriend-turned-informant Hazel Moore in a Capitol hotel room. The notorious arrest videos made relentless airtime, with Barry muttering: "Goddamn setup . . . I'll be goddamn . . . bitch set me up." Barry had been active in local Washington politics since the 1970s, and became mayor in 1979. Although the embarrassing drug bust cost him a six-month prison sentence that took him out of a campaign for re-election in 1991, the stubborn politico ran for the District Council in 1992, won the mayor's office back in 1995, and continues as a councilman for the District of Columbia. Maybe there's the slimmest of chances that Barry is the extremely rare politician who's actually a semi-decent guy who overcame doing something incredibly stupid.

The Peabrain Politico Dictionary

Electoral college: Where electricians
get their education

Strategic Arms Limitation Talks: Deciding
who to shoot

Press Secretary: She who does the ironing

Heels on Wheels

If politicians had cars named after them,
what would they be?

Tom Delay: Dodge Indictment

Ted Kennedy: Honda Pub Crawler

Jesse Helms: Nissan Repulsive

Just Say *Duh!*

Serving five terms as Speaker of the House of Texas Representatives, Gib Lewis is a well-known political figure in the Lone Star state. As most politicians do, Lewis has more than a few controversies on his record, including being indicted and convicted of violating financial disclosure laws in 1992. But it's his vernacular—or lack thereof—that makes him memorable. Over the years, Lewis belted out legendary remarks such as: "There's a lot of uncertainty that's not clear in my mind," and "This is unparalyzed in the state's history," and the ever popular "I cannot tell you how grateful I am—I am filled with humidity." Remind you of anyone? But the mother of all gaffes was the simple phrase: "And now, will y'all stand and be recognized." Why was *that* a major blunder? Lewis said it to a group of wheelchair-bound individuals on Disability Day. Must be something in the Texas water . . .

Republican Numbnuts

Sure signs you're dealing with a harebrained elected Republican.

They think "proletariat" is a French cheese.

They send the CIA a list of their neighbors they suspect are communists.

Bumper Snickers!

OUR SENATOR CAN DRINK YOUR HONOR STUDENT UNDER THE TABLE!
The entire population of Massachusetts

I NEVER THOUGHT I'D MISS REAGAN.
Mikhail Gorbachev

WHY IS TED KENNEDY INTERESTED IN MIDDLE EAST AFFAIRS?

HE THINKS THE GAZA STRIP IS A TOPLESS BAR.

Film at Eleven

Favorite films of the truly daft.

Ronald Reagan: *Murder on the Disorient Express*

Jesse Helms: *A Midsummer Night's Scream*

Scooter Libby: *The Spy Who Shoved Me*

Bumper Snickers!

TO SUCCEED IN POLITICS, IT'S NECESSARY TO RISE ABOVE YOUR PRINCIPLES.
Karl Rove

HONK IF YOU'VE SLEPT WITH CLINTON!
Monica Lewinsky

Heaven and Hell

John F. Kennedy and the Pope both die on the same day, but a paperwork snafu accidentally sends the Pope to hell and Kennedy to heaven. Meeting with Satan, the Pontiff explains that there must be some kind of mistake and asks him to check it out. After consulting with God, they both realize the clerical error and agree to make the switch. Satan leads the holy man to an escalator and waves goodbye. Up in heaven, God does the same thing, shaking Kennedy's hand before he disappears into the depths of hell. Halfway down, the two men cross paths. "I'm so sorry about the mix-up, my child," says the Pope. Kennedy brushes it off. "No problem Your Holiness. These things happen." The Pope thanks him and then relates how ready he is to finally see heaven. "Why so thrilled?" says Kennedy. "It's not that exciting." The Pope shakes his head. "My child. I've waited my entire life to meet the Virgin Mary. It will be the defining moment of my life." Kennedy grins, then whispers in the Pope's ear, "I'm sorry, Your Holiness. But you're too late."

Politics Explained

Fascism: *You have four pigs. The government takes them and triples the price of pork. You start an underground rebellion.*

American Democracy: *Your brood sow has six piglets. The government takes three as a capital gains tax and sends one of them to a foreign country.*

Dictatorship: *You have two pigs. They're declared subversive, confiscated, and slaughtered in public. The dictator has a private barbecue.*

Republican: *You have four pigs and your neighbors don't. Ha. Ha. Ha.*

Democrat: *You have four pigs. You righteously demand that the government provides your less fortunate neighbors with pigs. You hide yours in the attic.*

Communism: *You have four pigs. The Kremlin confiscates them for the upper classes, and you pay exorbitant prices for bacon on the black market.*

Socialism: *You have four pigs that become mascots for your hippie commune.*

Anarchism: *You have four pigs. All your neighbors show up in the middle of the night and claim them for themselves.*

Arkansas politics: *You have four pigs. And one of 'em is really cute.*

The Proverbial Politician

You can lead a candidate to voters,
but you can't make him think.

Bumper Snickers!

TOO CLOSE FOR MISSILES.
SWITCHING TO GUNS.
Donald Rumsfeld

HAVE YOU BITCH SLAPPED AN
ENVIRONMENTALIST TODAY?
Secretary of the Interior Dirk
Kempthorne

Just Say *Duh!*

Few politicians have headline making debacles involving major vegetables, unless of course you consider George Bush's ridiculous hatred of broccoli or feel the entire U.S. Congress are a bunch of overcooked rutabagas. For Jim Rodgers, Lord Mayor of Belfast, Ireland, an encounter with a giant tomato proved extremely traumatizing. In September 2007, during a Botanic Gardens gourmet garden event, Rodgers decided to accommodate photographers by leapfrogging over council worker Lorraine Mallon, who at the time was dressed as a giant tomato. After several successful jumps, the sixty-five-year-old Rodgers went for another leap and that's when things got dicey. Rodgers knee hit Mallon's head and the saucy little pseudo-veggie slipped a disc. *Oops!* Rodgers was devastated by the incident and the unintentional injury inflicted on the peaceable produce. Perhaps at the next garden event, he should try his hand at squash.

Democratic Dimwits

Sure signs you're dealing with a dunderheaded
elected Democrat.

They think Ralph Nader is
a very sensible guy.

They are firm in their beliefs that there is no
such thing as Nipplegate and that Janet
Jackson was framed.

Film at Eleven

Favorite films of the truly daft.

Dick Cheney: *Raging Bullcrap*

Gary Hart: *For Your Thighs Only*

Clarence Thomas: *Saving My Privates*

Democracy Inaction

For the Bush administration, Alberto Gonzales seemed like the perfect choice for Attorney General of the United States. After all, he'd been Bush's White House counsel and his general counsel in Texas. Not long after being sworn in on February 14, 2005, Gonzales began self-destructing after failing to explain his influence in the questionable dismissal of several U.S. attorneys throughout the country—attorneys who reportedly held views counter to those of the White House. That political snafu all by itself resulted in Congressional calls to oust the Attorney General, but things rapidly snowballed when Gonzales played a major role in the renewal of the Patriot Act, with resulting reductions in American freedom from governmental snooping into personal affairs. Gonzales sealed his own fate after initially refusing to answer to a Congressional inquiry. When Gonzales finally testified, his statements about the National Security Agency's surveillance programs quickly came under fire, particularly after his comments were refuted by FBI Director Robert Mueller. *Oops!* Can anyone spell "perjury"? After going from the frying pan to the fire, Gonzales finally jumped off the stove and turned in his resignation, leaving office on September 17, 2007.

The Peabrain Politico Dictionary

Laissez faire: A ménage à trois

Joint committees: Ben Gay testers

Smear campaign: What women get every six months

Stupid Says . . .

"We are not without accomplishment. We have managed to distribute poverty equally."

—Former Vietnamese Foreign Minister Nguyen Co Thatch

Republican Numbnuts

Sure signs you're dealing with a harebrained elected Republican.

When you say the word "Marx," they think Groucho.

They believe that insurance companies should run the national health care system.

Sex, Lies, and Videotape

Sexual predators often go to incredible lengths to establish positions of trust and authority with the express purpose of exploiting young men and under-age boys. Jim West took the concept to extremes during stints as a sheriff's deputy, Boy Scout leader, state legislator, and of all things, the mayor of Spokane, Washington. West's habit of using his political position to lure young men through Internet chat rooms was uncovered by a Washington newspaper and resulted in a special election held in December 2005. The day the votes were counted, West was tossed out of office. Curiously, West's activities were investigated by the FBI, and he was cleared of legal charges in February 2006. West died from complications of cancer the following December, and hopefully, part of the legacy of power abuse by political sharks died with him.

WHAT WAS GEORGE BUSH'S
STANCE ON
ROE VS. WADE?

HE REALLY DIDN'T CARE
HOW PEOPLE ESCAPED
FROM NEW ORLEANS.

Promises, Promises . . .

WHAT THE CANDIDATE PROMISES:
To find weapons of mass destruction.

WHAT THE ELECTED OFFICIAL DOES:
Claims they do exist—they're just in a really good hiding place.

Heels on Wheels

If politicians had cars named after them, what would they be?

Barbara Bush: Dodge Status

Richard Nixon: Pontiac Grand Scam

John F. Kennedy: Fiat Coup de Grace

Republican Numbnuts

Sure signs you're dealing with a harebrained elected Republican.

They believe themselves to be true patriots but can't recite any constitutional amendments.

They think metrosexuals are trannies who live in urban areas.

Promises, Promises . . .

WHAT THE CANDIDATE PROMISES:
He'll legalize same sex marriage.

WHAT THE ELECTED OFFICIAL DOES:
Votes against same sex marriage and then has an affair with his male campaign manager.

Politicos in the Pokey

Sometimes it seems that law enforcement stings designed to ferret out unscrupulous politicians could be likened to fishing for salmon in a hatchery pond with a sack of fish food and a trolling net. Just toss in the bait and scoop 'em out. In one case, seven Tennessee lawmakers fell for a scheme nicknamed Operation Tennessee Waltz in which agents posed as representatives of a phony electronics equipment recycling company called "E-Cycle," seeking to expand business operations into Tennessee. A series of bribes were paid to the indicted lawmakers for introducing legislation promoting the non-existent company. The highest bribe was $55,000 paid to Representative John Ford, who also faced the most serious charges, including witness intimidation. In August 2007, Ford was sentenced to more than five years in federal prison. One piece of evidence was a videotape that showed him stuffing $10,000 in $100 bills into his suit pockets. The incredible stupidity of political shenanigans was highlighted by a statement Ford made on the tape. When agents asked him if he wanted to count the money, he replied: "I ain't trying to count. I trust you."

The Wicked Witch of the East Award

When it comes to rabid right-wing commentator Ann Coulter there's no grey area. You love her or you hate her. What's to despise, you ask? Let's begin with the garbage she spewed after 9/11. In a September 12 column for the *National Review*, she asserted her opinion on dealing with terrorists: "We should invade their countries, kill their leaders, and convert them to Christianity." Uh huh. Good plan. She later turned her attention to the widows of 9/11 victims, writing in her book *Godless: The Church of Liberalism*: "These broads are millionaires, lionized on TV and in articles about them, reveling in their status as celebrities and stalked by grief-arazzis. I have never seen people enjoying their husbands' deaths so much." In March 2007, Coulter blew the mercury clear out of the vile meter during the Conservative Political Action Conference. Showing true crass, Coulter cut loose: "I was going to have a few comments on the other Democratic presidential candidate John Edwards, but it turns out you have to go into rehab if you use the word 'faggot,' so I—so kind of an impasse, can't really talk about Edwards." Gotta love the First Amendment, eh?

Democratic Dimwits

Sure signs you're dealing with a dunderheaded elected Democrat.

Their iPod consists of Joan Baez, Joni Mitchell, and Jefferson Airplane.

They don't have a problem clear-cutting forests, but God forbid any spotted owls lose their homes!

The Peabrain Politico Dictionary

Gun control: Using both hands and aiming carefully

House Whips: An S&M collection

Patriot Act: A preemptive attack on civil liberties to keep terrorists from destroying them first

Presidential Pinheads

More than a few American presidents were enthusiastic imbibers, one of whom was Franklin Pierce, who's often cited as one of the worst leaders the U.S. has ever had. Coincidentally, George Dubya was busted in Maine in 1976 for DUI and his loyal henchman, Dick Cheney, was busted twice for DWI (as it was then called) in the 1960s in Wyoming. But we digress. Pierce, the fourteenth President of the United States, was a notorious alcoholic. In 1856, after losing the Democratic nomination, Pierce allegedly stated that "there's nothing left to do but get drunk." And it appears he did—a lot. Luckily for the former Prez, drunk driving laws weren't yet in existence, because during one drunken binge he drove his horse-drawn carriage over a female pedestrian. Pierce died of cirrhosis of the liver in 1869, and is no doubt still coveting that big Presidential mini-bar in the sky.

Bumper Snickers!

DON'T PLAY STUPID WITH ME.
I'M BETTER AT IT!
Dan Quayle

DON'T DRINK AND DRIVE, YOU MIGHT
SPILL YOUR MARTINI.
Ted Kennedy

The Proverbial Politician

People who live in White Houses
shouldn't throw stones.

Full of It

A man was walking down a rural country road when he saw a young lad building something. Moving closer, he noticed the boy using cow manure to construct a figure. "Wow," said the man. "That's quite a project. What are you building?" The boy grinned. "I'm making Bill Maher out of manure!" The man shook his head. "Uh. I hate to be nosy, but why Bill Maher?" The youngster giggled. "Well, sir. I haven't got enough manure to make Rush Limbaugh."

Nitwits in the News

In a fantasy world, politics would be all about honesty, integrity, and performing public services purely for the health, wealth, and happiness of the citizenry. In real life, it's more about power, money, and keeping one's skeletons securely in one's closet. Former South Carolina Senator Strom Thurmond had one whopper of a skeleton that didn't emerge from hiding until after his death in June 2003 at the age of 100. That secret was seventy-eight-year-old Essie Mae Washington-Williams, Thurmond's illegitimate daughter, who was born in 1925 when Thurmond was twenty-two. Her mother was sixteen-year-old Carrie Butler, a maid working for the Thurmond family in South Carolina. What makes the secret so scandalous? In 1948, Thurmond made a run for the presidency on the States Rights Party ticket. Known as the "Dixiecrats," the party adamantly opposed civil rights programs, believing fervently in racial segregation. Carrie Butler was African American. To his credit, Thurmond didn't abandon his daughter, meeting her for the first time when she was sixteen and paying for her education and needs throughout her adulthood. But regardless of his eventual shift to Republicanism, it's a big skeleton for a rabid segregationist.

Film at Eleven

Favorite films of the truly daft.

Sandy Berger: *The Wrest Wing*

John Edwards: *It's a Wonderful Wife*

Marion Barry: *The Greatest Blow on Earth*

The Peabrain Politico Dictionary

Ex parte: Living it up with a former spouse

Nuclear weapons: Inventions designed
to end all inventions

Senate committees: Individuals who do
nothing by themselves and meet to agree
that nothing can be done together

Stupid Says . . .

"Gerald Ford is a communist."

—Ronald Reagan, having meant to call
Ford a congressman

Promises, Promises . . .

WHAT THE CANDIDATE PROMISES:
*That all women have the right to choose what
they do with their bodies.*

WHAT THE ELECTED OFFICIAL DOES:
*Immediately overturns Roe vs. Wade, closes all
clinics, and outlaws the "morning after" pill.*

Evolution of a Moron

66 Politics gives guys so much power that they tend to behave badly around women. And I hope I never get into that. 99

> —Bill Clinton, to a female friend while he was a Rhodes scholar at Oxford

66 I did not have sexual relations with that woman, Miss Lewinsky. 99

> —President Bill Clinton

66 I've learned not to put things in my mouth that are bad for me. 99

> —Monica Lewinsky discussing her miraculous Jenny Craig weight-loss on **Larry King Live**

The Proverbial Politician

Hell hath no fury like a mistress scorned.

Nitwits in the News

In yet another classic example of wasting our hard earned tax dollars, Virginia state delegate Lionel Spruill is at it again. In 2005, the legislative lummox introduced a bill to outlaw baggy pants. Yes, baggy pants that—*gasp*—expose people's underwear. But that's not the latest ban *du jour*. This time it's rubber testicles. Yep. Big ol' honkin' rubber testes that a few drivers have seen fit to attach to their bumpers or trailer hitches. According to Spruill, the bouncy distraction was brought to his attention by a constituent who was forced to explain what they were to his young daughter who saw them dangling from a trailer hitch. Spruill decided to take up the cause, and in January 2008, introduced the bill to the Virginia General Assembly. If Spruill gets his way, folks who have the balls to hang a set of . . . uh . . . balls from their bumper would be fined $250 and charged with a misdemeanor. Dare we say the proposed bill is just plain nuts?

Stupid Says . . .

66Traditionally, most of Australia's imports come from overseas.99

—Former Australian cabinet minister
Keppel Enderbery

Democratic Dimwits

Sure signs you're dealing with a dunderheaded elected Democrat.

They don't worry about hitting on their interns because Bill got away with it.

They assume when you say "political royalty" you're referring to the Kennedy family.

The Peabrain Politico Dictionary

Polls: A device used by strippers to gauge the opinions of politicians

Diplomat: A person who can tell you to go to hell in such a way you look forward to the trip

Political office: A place to relax from a strenuous social life

Promises, Promises . . .

WHAT THE CANDIDATE PROMISES:
To increase Social Security benefits.

WHAT THE ELECTED OFFICIAL DOES:
Mandates an additional 25 percent tax on Social Security earnings.

Just Say *Duh*!

Okay. We're just going to come right out and say it. Peter Gloystein is a scumbag. As the economics minister and deputy leader of the well-to-do German state of Bremen, you'd think Gloystein would've had the ability to show public decorum. Not a chance. In May of 2005, Gloystein, who is a member of the Christian Democrats (CDU), was a guest at the opening of Bremen Wine Week. In front of an enthusiastic crowd, Gloystein callously turned to a man near the podium and poured a bottle of bubbly all over him, stating: "Here's something for you to drink as well." As it happened, the shocked recipient of Gloystein's dousing was Udo Oelschläger, a poor homeless man who tearfully asked who Gloystein was and why he was pouring wine on him. No doubt at the persistence of the horrified revelers, Gloystein tried to offer Oelschläger money, his Montblanc pen, even a night in a fancy schmancy hotel, all of which was rebuked. "You offended me and wanted to make me look like an idiot," Oelschläger reportedly said. The incident resulted in Gloystein resigning and Oelschläger pressing charges. Perhaps a life sentence for the Minister of Condescension in a homeless shelter would be appropriate, eh?

The Proverbial Politician

A handful of vetoes helps the reticent go down.

Film at Eleven

Favorite films of the truly daft.

John McCain: *Gone with the Windbag*

Bob Allen: *The Little Barmaid*

Tom DeLay: *Guess Who's Coming to Rikers?*

Home of the Free

The top five reasons democracy and capitalism work in America.

1. Department store Santas are legal, but the Easter Bunny must now be called the "Holiday Bunny."
2. Drive-thru ATM machines have instructions written in Braille.
3. Inflation is solved by selling hot dogs ten to a package and buns in packs of eight.
4. Campaign donations are write-offs, but pharmaceuticals for the uninsured are not.
5. Janet Jackson's hooter is indecent, but kids are just a mouse click away from Internet porn.

Heels on Wheels

If politicians had cars named after them, what would they be?

Gary Condit: Jeep Strangler

Chuck Schumer: Oldsmobile Bravado

Charleton Heston: Mercury Ruger

Stupid Says . . .

66 We are trying to change the 1974 Constitution, whenever that was passed."

—Louisiana state representative
Donald Kennard

Democratic Dimwits

Sure signs you're dealing with a dunderheaded
elected Democrat.

They think the three strike rule should only
apply in baseball.

They think Rush Limbaugh is just an
"entertainer."

The Marie Antoinette Award

As matriarch of the Bush clan Barbara Bush looks like a sweet old granny, but her overwhelming sense of entitlement punctuated by an extreme "let 'em eat cake" complex makes her a very ugly figure in the Texas tyranny. In September 2005 after Hurricane Katrina, Bush spoke about the unfortunate refugees holed up in the Houston Astrodome. "What I'm hearing, which is sort of scary, is they all want to stay in Texas," she said. "Everyone is so overwhelmed by the hospitality. And so many of the people in the arena here, you know, were underprivileged anyway, so this is working very well for them." *Pfft.* Further depravity ensued in 2006, when she donated an undisclosed sum of money to the Bush-Clinton Katrina fund. Were there strings attached? You bet. She instructed the funds be spent at an educational software company owned by her son, Neil Bush. And lest we forget, her 2003 *Good Morning America* interview about American soldiers dying in Iraq: "Why should we hear about body bags and deaths? Oh, I mean, it's not relevant. So why should I waste my beautiful mind on something like that?"

Snake Oil Subterfuge

The top five indicators that you're dealing with a
stupid politician.

1. They equate the term "dirty laundry" with
   finding a great dry cleaner.
2. When you ask them how they plan on solv-
   ing global warming, they suggest reducing
   hot air emissions by cutting Congressional
   sessions to one day a week.
3. When you bring up the subject of capital
   punishment they swear they only write in
   lowercase letters.
4. When you mention illegal aliens they tell
   you they don't believe there's life on other
   planets.
5. They suddenly start saying "y'all" and eating grits when campaigning in the South.

Film at Eleven

Favorite films of the truly daft.

Mark Foley: *Dead Man Talking*

Donald Rumsfeld: *Patriot Blame*

J. Edgar Hoover: *The Accidental Anarchist*

Politicos in the Pokey

When it comes to politicians and sex scandals, most are pretty mundane compared to the disgusting creepiness of former Congressman Donald Lukens. Lukens was indicted and convicted in 1989 for contributing to the delinquency of a child and sentenced to thirty days in jail. What did Lukens do to deserve it? Hold on to your hats. It turned out that Lukens had paid for sex with the teenaged girl on numerous occasions, beginning when she was just *thirteen*. How child molestation could be construed as delinquency is beyond us. Lukens grudgingly resigned from Congress in 1990 under intense pressure after he was accused of fondling a female elevator operator at the Capitol, and six years later he was convicted of bribery and conspiracy charges related to investigations of the House Banking scandal. Lukens was slapped with a thirty-month sentence in federal prison. Should have been thirty lifetimes in hell for this dirtbag.

The Proverbial Politician

Ask me more questions and I'll tell you more lies.

Bumper Snickers!

IF AT FIRST YOU DO SUCCEED, TRY NOT
TO LOOK ASTONISHED.
Barack Obama

GROW YOUR OWN DOPE. PLANT A BUSH.
The Green Party

Sex, Lies, and Videotape

Denying adulterous affairs is nothing unusual for U.S. Congressmen, but when foul play enters the mix, a shady relationship can quickly take on much darker undertones. After the disappearance of Chandra Levy, an intern for the Federal Bureau of Prisons in Washington, D.C., just days after her twenty-fourth birthday in April 2001, police discovered that Levy was acquainted with California Congressman Gary Condit. During two investigative conversations with police, the married Condit acknowledged that he and Levy were "friends." Over the following months, allegations that Condit and Levy were more closely involved were met with denials, but on July 6, Levy's aunt dropped bombshell news. Levy had confided that she and Condit were having an affair. After that, national attention fell squarely on Condit, and while he was never officially a person of interest in the case, public sentiment and suspicion dogged him for the rest of his term. His political career imploded when he lost his March 2002 bid for re-election by a wide margin. Chandra Levy's remains were discovered nearly two months later in a Washington, D.C., park on May 22, 2002. The victim of a homicide, her killer remains unknown.

Mix and Mingle: Peabrain Politico Anagrams

a. Tony Blair

b. Gary Condit

c. Vladimir Putin

d. Marion Barry

e. Ralph Nader

f. Jesse Ventura

g. Tom Delay

h. Saddam Hussein

i. Newt Gingrich

j. Jerry Falwell

1. LAMED TOY

2. BRAINY LOT

3. RAP HANDLER

4. RAW FLYERJELL

5. RETCHING WING

6. DIRTY CONGA

7. BINARY ARMOR

8. TRIVIA DINLUMP

9. SEVERE JAUNTS

10. UNASHAMED DISS

Answers:
1-g, 2-a, 3-e, 4-
j, 5-i, 6-b, 7-d,
8-c, 9-f, 10-h

Presidential Pinheads

Though it's certain there are a few presidents out there who've received tickets while on the road, only one is on record as actually having received a speeding ticket. Ulysses S. Grant, America's eighteenth president, served from 1869 to 1877, and during that time he was indeed pulled over by a police officer for exceeding the speed limit in his horse-drawn carriage! Some stories say the officer didn't recognize the President and gave him a ticket with a $20 fine. Many others say that upon recognizing Grant, the officer didn't want to give him a ticket, but Grant insisted the officer fulfill his duty. Imagine that. A politician who refuses to weasel out of an infraction. They don't make 'em like that anymore.

The Peabrain Politico Dictionary

Inalienable rights: Welfare for illegal immigrants

Incumbent: A motionless immovable object

Nuclear disarmament: Finding better hiding places for weapons of mass destruction

HOW MANY POLITICIANS DOES IT TAKE TO CHANGE A

LIGHT BULB?

TWO.

ONE TO PROMISE HE'LL DO IT BETTER THAN ANYONE ELSE AND THE OTHER TO OBSCURE

HOW IT'S DONE.

Democracy Inaction

Evan Mecham, former governor of Arizona, was a man with the unique capacity to become the first U.S. governor in history to face removal from office through the triple threat of a felony indictment, a recall election, *and* impeachment. Mecham got the ball rolling by canceling the state's Martin Luther King Day, saying that the famous civil rights activist "doesn't deserve a holiday." To a group of black community leaders, the soon to be *ex*-governor said: "You folks don't need another holiday. What you folks need are jobs." Well, *that* was succinct. The public backlash was instantaneous and effective, as conventions were cancelled and Arizona's tourist industry went down the tubes. Finding himself in a hole, Mecham responded by continuing to dig, saying: "I've got black friends. I employ black people. I employ them because they're the best people who applied for the cotton-picking job." Having painted a bull's eye on his own back, Mecham was investigated for criminal financial dealings, impeached, and tossed out of office by the State Senate on April 4, 1988.

Democratic Dimwits

Sure signs you're dealing with a dunderheaded elected Democrat.

They think it's okay to cheat on their wife, but *not* their mistress.

They have an "Earth First" bumper sticker on their $80,000 Cadillac Escalade.

Bumper Snickers!

IF YOU CAN'T DAZZLE THEM WITH BRIL-
LIANCE, BAFFLE THEM WITH BULLSHIT.
Mike Huckabee

DO I LOOK LIKE A FREAKIN'
PEOPLE PERSON?
Jesse Helms

Heels on Wheels

If politicians had cars named after them,
what would they be?

Pat Robertson: Mitsubishi Excessive

George Dubya Bush: Dodge Draft

Alberto Gonzales: Honda Hindsight

The Proverbial Politician

Ask not what you can do for your voters,
but what you can't do for your country.

Lost in Translation

WHAT YOU SAY:
I'm boycotting the next election.

WHAT A STUPID POLITICIAN HEARS:
Thanks to Viagra I can get an erection.

Republican Numbnuts

Sure signs you're dealing with a harebrained elected Republican.

They think Hollywood liberals are a bunch of rich hippies who don't have the right to an opinion.

They insist Tom DeLay, Bob Livingston, Bob Packwood, Antonio Gonzales, and Newt Gingrich are pillars of the community, but Ted Kennedy should be in the pokey for Chappaquiddick.

Stupid Says . . .

66If somebody has a bad heart, they can plug this jack in at night as they go to bed and it will monitor their heart throughout the night. And the next morning, when they wake up dead, there'll be a record.99

—Former FCC Chairman Mark Fowler

Bumper Snickers!

I GAVE UP SEX, DRUGS, AND BOOZE. IT
WAS THE WORST TWENTY MINUTES
OF MY LIFE.
Marion Barry

I'M OUT OF MY MIND. I'LL BE BACK IN
FIVE MINUTES.
John McCain

The Peabrain Politico Dictionary

Eurocentrism: Making change for
foreign currency

Hanging chad: Capital punishment

Plausible deniability: Convincing your constituents that your mistress is only your
secretary

Nitwits in the News

In what can only be described as hysterical irony, Nebraska Senator Ernie Chambers is suing God. Yes, God. And before we mention specifics, it must be said that he's filing the suit to prove that anyone can file a lawsuit against anyone they choose. Filed in September 2007, Chambers' suit seeks a permanent injunction against the Lord, ordering he "cease harmful activities and the making of terroristic threats." The suit also accuses God of causing floods, hurricanes, earthquakes, tornados, famine, droughts, genocidal wars, and "pestilential plagues." Chambers, who's not a religious individual, asserts in his suit that the defendant is "Omnipresent," and despite contacting God on numerous occasions, he hasn't received a response. Line forms to the left for everyone wishing to sue God for creating WWE wrestling, *Wife Swap*, Paris Hilton, and Brussels sprouts.

The Proverbial Politician

Fool me once, the blame's on you.
Fool me twice, the blame's **still** on you.

Film at Eleven

Favorite films of the truly daft.

Richard Daly: *The Wrong Stuff*

Bill Clinton: *The Silence of the Gams*

Karl Rove: *Lord of the Rings: The Two Cowards*

Lost in Translation

WHAT YOU SAY:
I can't afford medical care.

WHAT A STUPID POLITICIAN HEARS:
My insurance premiums are very fair.

WHY AREN'T WHITE HOUSE EMPLOYEES ALLOWED

COFFEE BREAKS?

IT TAKES TOO LONG TO RETRAIN THEM.

Promises, Promises . . .

WHAT THE CANDIDATE PROMISES:
*That no child will be left behind when
getting an education.*

WHAT THE ELECTED OFFICIAL DOES:
*Cuts the education budget by 50 percent, cuts
teachers' salaries by 40 percent, and raises
college entrance fees.*

The Proverbial Politician

A constituent saved is a constituent burned.

Film at Eleven

Favorite films of the truly daft.

Hillary Clinton: *Mrs. Clinton
Goes to Washington*

George Dubya Bush: *The Man
Who Knew Too Little*

Deep Throat: *An Inconvenient Sleuth*

Mix and Mingle: Dimwit Democrat Anagrams

a. Barack Obama

b. Nancy Pelosi

c. Ted Kennedy

d. Dianne Feinstein

e. Tip O'Neill

f. Tom Daschle

g. Chuck Schumer

h. John Kerry

i. Dick Gephardt

j. John Edwards

1. DEFINITE NANNIES

2. HORN JERKY

3. MUCK CHURCHES

4. CANINE PLOYS

5. DRAWN JOSHED

6. RACK DEPTHDIG

7. DYED NEKNET

8. LENTIL POI

9. KARMA BOACAB

10. ACHED MOLTS

Answers:
1-d, 2-h, 3-
g, 4-b, 5-j,
6-i, 7-c, 8-e,
9-a, 10-f

Bumper Snickers!

FLORIDA: HOME OF ELECTILE
DYSFUNCTION!
Al Gore

PUTTING THE "CON" IN CONSERVATIVE.
Former Congressman Duke Cunningham

Stupid Says . . .

❝I was provided with additional input that was radically different from the truth. I assisted in furthering that version.**❞**

—Colonel Oliver North during his
Iran-Contra testimony

Democratic Dimwits

Sure signs you're dealing with a dunderheaded elected Democrat.

They fully support Green Peace and P.E.T.A. but wear leather coats and eat meat and dolphin-based tuna.

They inhaled.

Promises, Promises . . .

WHAT THE CANDIDATE PROMISES:
To lift all sanctions and ease restrictions of television censorship.

WHAT THE ELECTED OFFICIAL DOES:
Tosses Janet Jackson and Justin Timberlake in the slammer.

Politicos in the Pokey

The investigation into the 2003 leak of CIA operative Valerie Plame's name to the press revealed the not so startling news that top Bush administration officials were bent on discrediting Plame's husband, former Ambassador Joseph Wilson. Wilson was highly critical of prewar intelligence on Iraq and accused the Bush camp of doctoring information concerning weapons of mass destruction. If discrediting Wilson was truly the intent of the exercise, the plan backfired miserably and destroyed the career of Dick Cheney's Chief of Staff, Lewis "Scooter" Libby, who bore the brunt of the fallout. Libby was indicted on five criminal counts, including one of obstruction of justice, and four of lying to cover up his involvement. He was convicted of four counts and sentenced to fines and thirty months in federal prison on June 5, 2007. After a failed appeal, Dubya commuted Libby's prison time, leaving the fines, supervised release, and community service portions of the sentence intact. There's little question that White House involvement in Plamegate didn't simply begin and end with Libby. Libby kept his mouth shut and became the proverbial sacrificial lamb for the administration.

The Peabrain Politico Dictionary

Lottery: A voluntary tax on people who are *really* bad at math

Absentee ballot: The Congressional vote

Fifth Amendment: A six pack to go with the Jack Daniels

Heels on Wheels

If politicians had cars named after them, what would they be?

Prince Charles: Oldsmobile Gutless

Trent Lott: GM SOB

Bob Livingston: Volkswagon Cabriolayme

Just Say *Duh*!

Picture if you will a bunch of guys celebrating a bachelor party by whooping it up at a strip club. The booze is flowing, the lap dancers are in full swing, and the bar tab is accelerating. At the end of the night a bill for $1,462 was delivered to the group, a credit card was used, and everyone went on their merry way. So what's the big problem, you ask? Well, the guy who paid the bill was Mike Smith, the mayor of the village of New Lenox, Illinois, and the card he used was the village credit card. That was in March of 2006. In February, Smith charged over $800 dollars at restaurants, often tipping $100. In January he dropped over $550 bucks, and in December he dropped over $1,300 at five swanky restaurants. Despite reimbursing the village fund for his personal spending, Smith was finally confronted about the strip club bill. His excuse? When the bill arrived none of his buddies had a credit card and the only one he had was the village's American Express card. Uh huh. We didn't believe it either.

WHAT DO YOU GET
WHEN YOU GIVE A
STUPID POLITICIAN A PENNY
FOR HIS THOUGHTS?

CHANGE.

Film at Eleven

Favorite films of the truly daft.

Roger Clinton: *The Beer Hunter*

Pat Robertson: *Citizen Lame*

Ann Coulter: *The Day of the Cackle*

Bumper Snickers!

PRACTICE SAFE GOVERNMENT.
USE KINGDOMS!
Rudy Giuliani

SPOTTED OWLS. THE OTHER WHITE MEAT.
Richard Pombo

Republican Numbnuts

Sure signs you're dealing with a harebrained elected Republican.

They'd rather hug a smokestack than hug a tree.

They think the Dixie Chicks are the devil's concubines.

Lost in Translation

WHAT YOU SAY:
What are you doing about illegal residents?

WHAT A STUPID POLITICIAN HEARS:
I think you should run for president.

Mistaken Identity

After their plane crashes, Al Gore, Barack Obama, and Hillary Clinton are sent to heaven and stand before God. Sitting in his throne, God turns to Gore. "So tell me Mr. Gore, what is it that you truly believe in?" Gore becomes serious. "I believe the polar ice caps are melting, that pollution is killing the environment, and that very soon the ozone will rip and we'll all die." God nods. "Very good. You may sit at my left." God then turns to Obama. "Mr. Obama, what do you truly believe in?" Obama looks grim. "My Lord, I believe that people should have the right to make their own decisions, not fall prey to some vast government control." God nods. "I concur. You may sit at my right." He then turns to Clinton. "Mrs. Clinton, if you may, please tell me what you truly believe in." Clinton grins. "I believe you're in my chair."

You Say Potato . . .

The top five differences between stupid Democrats and stupid Republicans.

1. Democrats have coronaries and have to declare medical bankruptcy. Republicans have foot fungus and no co-payment.
2. Democrats blame global warming on industrial pollution. Republicans blame it on Al Gore.
3. Democrats read *Rolling Stone*. Republicans claim they read the *Wall Street Journal*.
4. Democrats donate to charity to make themselves feel better. Republicans buy charities to make themselves feel better.
5. Democrats think Joan Baez was insightful. Republicans think she's a Vegas impersonator.

The Proverbial Politician

If at first you don't succeed, bribe, bribe again.

Bumper Snickers!

STRIP THE EARTH FIRST. THEN WE CAN MOVE ON TO THE OTHER PLANETS.
Rush Limbaugh

HAPPINESS IS GARY CONDIT'S FACE ON A MILK CARTON.
Robert and Susan Levy

Democratic Dimwits

Sure signs you're dealing with a dunderheaded elected Democrat.

They support raising the minimum wage because it'll increase taxable income.

They think *The Da Vinci Code* is historically accurate.

Just Say *Duh*!

Most folks would argue that in the world of politics, rhetoric is the name of the game. In reality, however, politics is about hypocrisy. Case in point, former Vice President Al Gore, a tireless campaigner for putting an end to global warming. He won an Oscar for the documentary *An Inconvenient Truth*. He even won a Nobel Peace Prize for his efforts. But does he practice what he preaches? Not so much. In 2007, Gore's global nagging came under fire when it was revealed that his fancy schmancy Tennessee mansion in the Belle Meade neighborhood of Nashville uses twenty times the amount of electricity and natural gas than the national average. What that means to us regular schmoes who do our best to conserve, is that around 10,656 kilowatt-hours is used annually by the average household. In 2006, Gore sucked up 221,000 kh with his average monthly electric bill running over $1,300, coupled with gas bills of almost $1,100 a month. In total, his 2006 combined gas and electric expenses were nearly $30,000. Global warming? Gore's hypocritical energy guzzling should come with a global warning!

Strangeness on a Train

The Clintons and Gores are taking a train to a Democratic convention. At the station the Clintons buy two tickets, but the Gores only purchase one. Bill is confounded. "Why did you only buy one ticket?" Al winks. "Observe and learn from the masters, Billy Boy." After boarding, the couples enter a stateroom. The Clintons take their assigned seats. The Gores cram into the small lavatory and shut the door just as the conductor arrives. He asks the Clintons for their tickets and they comply, then he knocks on the lavatory: "Ticket, please." The door opens and a single arm reaches out with a ticket. The conductor stamps it and moves on. Impressed by the Gores ingenuity, the Clintons decide to pull their own scheme. On the return trip, the Gores again buy one ticket. The Clintons don't buy any. "How do you expect to travel with no ticket?" says Al. Hillary winks. "Observe and learn from the masters, Global Boy." Once in their compartment, the Gores cram into the lavatory. The Clintons do the same in the adjoining room. After a few minutes, Hillary leaves their loo and approaches the Gores loo. "Tickets, please!"

Democracy Inaction

The 2000 presidential election came down to a last minute battle in Florida that thrust the state's Secretary of State, Katherine Harris, into the spotlight for all the wrong reasons. Harris had oversight over the state's presidential election, which was quite the coincidence, considering she was also George Dubya's Florida campaign co-chair. Before the election, Harris hired a private firm in her role as Secretary of State to search state voter registrations to weed out convicted felons who were ineligible to vote. When election day came, thousands of voters were turned away at the polls, but as it turned out the vast majority had never been convicted of felonies. The supposition that most of those voters were Democrats singled out by Harris' involvement was impossible to prove, but Harris was skewered as a blatant partisan. Bush won the election and Harris capitalized on her expected Republican Party repayment of loyalty by running for the U.S. Senate in 2006. Then the wheels fell off her cart. Controversy over sketchy campaign contributions snowballed into a retraction of Republican leader support, and Harris' campaign sank like a rock. Some might call it bad luck. We call it karma.

Stupid Says . . .

66We don't want balloons, the plastics, the horror!99

—Green Party media coordinator Doug Heller

Republican Numbnuts

Sure signs you're dealing with a harebrained elected Republican.

They love Dubya cuz that's how they pronounce the letter "W."

They think nothing of paying $5,000 for a hamburger at a fundraiser, but balk at raising the minimum wage for fast-food workers.

Promises, Promises . . .

WHAT THE CANDIDATE PROMISES:
To start enforcing the death penalty in an effort to eliminate prison overcrowding.

WHAT THE ELECTED OFFICIAL DOES:
Abolishes the death penalty and releases 40,000 mentally impaired felons onto the streets.

The Peabrain Politico Dictionary

Presidential primary: George Dubya's twenty-minute potty break

Bolshevik: A cold Russian soup

Full faith and credit: Praying that interest rates don't go up

Sex, Lies, and Videotape

Given their highly public positions, politicians seldom fail to amaze normal people in their attempts to hide illicit affairs—until those dalliances blow up in their faces. Former New Jersey Governor James McGreevey's decision to come out of the closet was one case in point. Married and the father of two children, McGreevey made a bombshell announcement in August 2004, by admitting to an adulterous affair with a man and resigning his position as governor. McGreevey's confession, although ostensibly offered as a cathartic revelation, came about as former security aide Golan Cipel prepared to launch a sexual harassment suit. McGreevey's supremely contrite and purportedly poignant speech garnered praise from gay rights groups and sympathetically inclined state and federal officials, but in light of Golan's impending lawsuit, it's obvious that McGreevey had backed himself into a corner with no other way out. For shame . . .

HOW IS A STUPID POLITICIAN LIKE A CHARACTER ACTOR?

WHEN HE SHOWS CHARACTER, HE'S ACTING.

Lost in Translation

WHAT YOU SAY:
You're as dumb as a box of rocks.

WHAT A STUPID POLITICIAN HEARS:
I fully support your invading Iraq.

Bumper Snickers!

THE LAST TIME PEOPLE LISTENED TO A
BUSH THEY WANDERED THROUGH THE
DESERT FOR FORTY YEARS.
Vladimir Putin

HOW MANY LIVES PER GALLON?
The United States Senate

Riddle Me This

After years of American spy operations and false intelligence information being disseminated, Osama Bin Laden got really frustrated with the Bush administration questioning if he was still alive, so he decided to send Dubya a handwritten letter. After mailing it to the White House, it arrived on Dubya's desk. Upon opening it, the Prez found a coded message which read:

37OHSSV 0773H

Thoroughly confused, Dubya sent it to Condoleezza Rice, who not being able to decipher it, gave it to the encryption department, the FBI, and the CIA—none of whom could decode the message. Then they sent it to MI-6, but even they couldn't make sense of it. Desperate, Dubya contacted the Mossad for help, and a Mossad agent sent an immediate response:

Tell Dubya he's holding the message upside down.

Heels on Wheels

If politicians had cars named after them,
what would they be?

George Bush: Mercury Vomit

Ronald Reagan: Dodge Tacomatose

Marion Barry: Honda Quaalude

Republican Numbnuts

Sure signs you're dealing with a harebrained
elected Republican.

They see no connection whatsoever to low
approval ratings and American economic
devastation as a result of war and financial
mishandlings.

They think acid rain is good for
cleaning asphalt.

The Proverbial Politician

It's not how you sin and abuse, it's how
you play to fame.

Politicos in the Pokey

During Tom DeLay's many years as a U.S. Congressman representing Texas, he developed a reputation as a lightning rod for the Republican Party, particularly by bullying fellow congressmen into blindly tagging along with George Dubya's Iraq agenda. DeLay frequently made the news with his involvement in high profile situations such as the unprecedented House emergency session that attempted to interfere with a Florida court's decision to remove the feeding tube from comatose accident victim Terri Schiavo in March 2005. DeLay was forced to apologize for comments he made in the aftermath of the Schiavo case—comments that suggested an endorsement of violence against judges who made unpopular rulings. In September 2005, DeLay was slapped with the first of several criminal indictments involving campaign funding, money laundering, and fraud. Although he vociferously denied any legal wrongdoing, the indictments cost him the powerful House Majority leadership and he pulled the plug on his congressional career in June 2006. DeLay is still awaiting trial on several criminal counts.

The Moronic Vernacular Vandal of the Millennium Award

As the undisputed king of verbal slaughter, George Dubya Bush has had so many oral snafus that he should wear a sign around his neck that says: "Over Four Billion Slurred." And that isn't much of an exaggeration. There are enough Dubya gaffes to fill a book that would rival *War and Peace*—something Dubya knows nothing about. Seriously. The guy says "nuke-you-lure." Need we say more?

❝You work three jobs? Uniquely American, isn't it? I mean, that is fantastic that you're doing that.❞

—In Omaha, Nebraska, to a divorced mother of three, including one son who is "mentally challenged"

❝There's an old saying in Tennessee, I know it's in Texas, probably in Tennessee, that says, fool me once, shame on, shame on you. Fool me, you can't get fooled again.❞

❝For every fatal shooting, there were roughly three non-fatal shootings. And, folks, this is unacceptable in America. It's just unacceptable. And we're going to do something about it.❞

66The thing that's wrong with the French is that they don't have a word for entrepreneur.99

66This is an impressive crowd—the haves and the have mores. Some people call you the elite—I call you my base.99

66You teach a child to read, and he or her will be able to pass a literacy test.99

66Our enemies are innovative and resourceful, and so are we. They never stop thinking about new ways to harm our country and our people, and neither do we.99

66I know how hard it is for you to put food on your family.99

66We need an energy bill that encourages consumption.99

66We are fully committed to working with both sides to bring the level of terror down to an acceptable level for both.99

66I know what I believe. I will continue to articulate what I believe and what I believe—I believe what I believe is right.99

66I am here to make an announcement that this Thursday, ticket counters and airplanes will fly out of Ronald Reagan Airport.99

Democratic Dimwits

Sure signs you're dealing with a dunderheaded elected Democrat.

They want to lobby for Bill Clinton getting his mug on Mt. Rushmore.

They cry every time they watch the movie *Dave*.

The Peabrain Politico Dictionary

Détente: A perfectly cooked pasta

Impeachment: Sending a fruit basket with a criminal indictment

Pigskin politics: Inviting the Dallas Cowboys cheerleaders to the White House

Lost in Translation

WHAT YOU SAY:
You have no public speaking skills.

WHAT A STUPID POLITICIAN HEARS:
When you give a speech I get chills.

Stupid Says . . .

"Dan would rather play golf than have sex any day.**"**

—Marilyn Quayle on her husband Dan

The Scariest Political Moment . . .
EVER

In May of 1991, President George Bush was experiencing an irregular heartbeat that was eventually diagnosed as atrial fibrillation and linked to his hyperthyroidism. The plan was to treat Bush's condition with medication, but after that proved unsuccessful, doctors decided it would be best to administer electrical shock. That, of course, meant that Bush would have to be anesthetized, thereby forcing his vice president to serve as president under the Twenty-Fifth Amendment. For those taking notes—that amounted to Dan Quayle becoming President Quayle. The prospect was horrifying and everyone in the nation—from infant to elder—began a collective panic attack that reverberated to such a cacophony that doctors kept feeding Bush meds until they finally kicked in.

The Proverbial Politician

Recession is the mother of retention.

Politicos in the Pokey

A Tennessee lobbyist made a big mistake in 1986 when he offered first-year legislator Randy McNally bribes to support bingo gambling bills in the Tennessee House of Representatives. After informing the FBI, McNally became the key player in a sting—dubbed *Operation Rocky Top*—laid out by the Feds and the Tennessee Bureau of Investigations to look into the depth of the shady dealings. Wearing a wire, McNally began accepting bribes to influence gambling legislation, racking up evidence for the ongoing operation that resulted in the convictions of dozens of participants. Among the casualties was Tennessee Secretary of State Gentry Crowell, whose office regulated bingo operations and lobbyist activities. Rather than face prosecution, the fifty-seven-year-old Crowell committed suicide, a fate suffered not long afterward by State Representative Ted Ray Miller after he was charged with soliciting and accepting a series of bribes from the Knox County Solid Waste Authority to influence a multi-million dollar incinerator proposal. In the aftermath of Operation Rocky Top, the lobbyists and state officials who gambled on bribery made a pretty stupid bet.

Brain Power

After years of being passed up for a promotion, a low-level executive decides he wants a brain transplant. In the hopes of raising his I.Q. he consults a transplant center, where he endures an extensive range of physical and mental tests. When the results are in, the doctor tells him he's approved for surgery, but warns him that the procedure is very expensive. "One ounce of a mathematician's brain is $20,000," says the physician. "An ounce of a CEO's brain is $50,000, and an ounce of a politician's brain is $200,000." The exec is shocked. "Wow. A single ounce from a politician's brain is $200,000? Why so much more than everyone else?" The physician shakes his head and whispers. "Have you any idea just how many politicians we need for an ounce of brains?"

Film at Eleven

Favorite films of the truly daft.

Strom Thurmond: *From Here to Paternity*
Joe McCarthy: *Nonsense and Reprehensibility*
Donald Lukens: *The Perv on the River of Denial*

The Peabrain Politico Dictionary

Autocrat: A mechanic

Totalitarianism: A rebellion against
Special K

Civil service: Performing one's duty without
having to attend anger management

Nitwits in the News

The practice of politicking is by its very nature a convoluted game. But there's one underlying current that has run the same course for centuries, and that's hypocrisy. Strom Thurmond, a staunch racist and segregationist, had an illegitimate child with an African American woman, and he kept it hidden from the public until his death. Idaho's former Republican Congresswoman Helen Chenoweth went all high and mighty on President Bill Clinton, calling for his resignation after the Lewinsky debacle. Days later, she admitted having an affair as a single woman with a married associate for six years. She apparently felt her affair was fine given that she asked for and received "God's forgiveness."

Georgia's former Republican Congressman Bob Barr was also on the Clinton witch-hunt, as one of the prosecutors in the President's Senate trial. A fervent pro-lifer, and proponent of the anti-gay Defense of Marriage Act, Barr once said: "The flames of hedonism, the flames of narcissism, the flames of self-centered morality are licking at the very foundation of our society, the family unit." Uh huh. Barr, who was married three times, was busted big time by Larry Flynt, who discovered that Barr's second wife had an abortion in 1983, and that during their divorce hearing he refused to answer questions about whether he cheated on her with the woman who became his third wife. And then there's that little matter of him being photographed licking whipped cream off strippers at his inaugural party.

Adding more fuel to the hypocrisy fire is California Congressman Ken Calvert, who in addition to being investigated by the FBI for shady land dealings, was arrested in 1993 for soliciting a prostitute. Caught red-handed by the police, Calvert was sitting in a parked car with his little constituent ready to take the podium. Calvert claimed he and his lady friend were "just talking," despite her head being in his lap. When asked, his strumpet admitted she was a heroin addict with a record for prostitution. For the record, Calvert is a Republican, a strong proponent of the Christian Coalition, and a member of the House Steering committee. Must be nice being holier than thou, eh?

Stupid Says . . .

"If you let that sort of thing go on, your bread and butter will be cut right out from under your feet.**"**

—Former British Foreign
Secretary Ernest Bevin

Promises, Promises . . .

WHAT THE CANDIDATE PROMISES:
To declassify hundreds of thousands of government documents and release them to the public.

WHAT THE ELECTED OFFICIAL DOES:
Blacks out a handful of grassy knoll conspiracy files and monitors everyone's cell phones.

Time Delay

When it comes to sheer stupidity courtesy the right wing conservative faction, we have Republican Tom DeLay to thank for a host of poisonous statements. Read 'em and weep:

66So many minority youths had volunteered that there was literally no room for patriotic folks like myself.99

—His classic excuse for avoiding serving in Vietnam.

66It's never been proven that air toxins are hazardous to people.99

66Now tell me the truth boys, is this kind of fun?99

—To three young Hurricane Katrina victims at the Houston Astrodome

66A woman can take care of the family. It takes a man to provide structure. To provide stability. Not that a woman can't provide stability, I'm not saying that . . . It does take a father, though."

Nitwits in the News

The story of John Edwards getting $400 haircuts during his fizzled 2008 presidential campaign raised national eyebrows, considering that so much of Edwards' rhetoric was directed at leveling the playing field of life for the ordinary average guys. The issue that occasionally got lost in the controversy was that it wasn't the ridiculously wealthy Edwards who was paying ridiculously exorbitant prices for celebrity stylist coiffures—it was his Democratic campaign committee that picked up the tab, frittering away contributions from wealthy supporters, self interest groups, and of course, ordinary average guys. Supercuts should picket *this* guy's mansion.

Stupid Says . . .

"I've always thought that underpopulated countries in Africa are vastly underpolluted."

—Former chief economist of the World Bank Lawrence Summers, explaining why we should export toxic wastes to Third World countries

Democratic Dimwits

Sure signs you're dealing with a dunderheaded elected Democrat.

They support abortion but think that capital punishment is cruel and unusual.

They'd rather own Birkenstock than ImClone stock.

The Peabrain Politico Dictionary

Joint Chiefs of Staff: Shepherds with arthritis

Pentagon: What Satanists covet

Bill of Rights: An invoice for the privilege of using Verizon

Just Say *Duh*!

The irony of the term "political correctness" is that while we struggle to keep up with appropriate verbiage, stupid politicians pay little attention to the latest verbal standards. In May 2006, White House Press Secretary Tony Snow weaseled his way around the phrase "hug the tar baby," and when called out, explained that "we could trace it back to American lore." Next up were two frontrunners for the 2008 Republican presidential nomination, both proving once again that politicians don't learn from anyone else's mistakes. During a fundraiser in Ames, Iowa, in July 2006, Massachusetts' then-Governor Mitt Romney was discussing Boston's troublesome Big Dig construction project when he said: "The best thing politically would be to stay as far away from that tar baby as I can." Fast forward to March 2007, when John McCain held a town hall meeting in Cedar Falls, Iowa. During a Q&A session he said: "For me to stand here before all these people and say that I'm going to declare divorces invalid because someone feels that they weren't treated fairly in court, we are getting into a, uh, uh, tar baby of enormous proportions." It would appear the Republican faction needs to attend PC school *again*.

Promises, Promises . . .

What the candidate promises:

To reinforce broken levees in low lying metropolitan areas.

What the elected official does:

Sends a few trucks filled with water wings to thousands of flood victims.

Bumper Snickers!

I PLEAD CONTEMPORARY INSANITY.
Larry Craig

I'M NOT AS STUPID AS YOUR PRESIDENT
THINKS I AM.
Tony Blair

Film at Eleven

Favorite films of the truly daft.

Alberto Gonzales: *To Kill a Mocking Third*

Katherine Harris: *Chariots of Liars*

Oliver North: *Duty and the Deceased*

Republican Numbnuts

Sure signs you're dealing with a harebrained elected Republican.

They always confuse Lenin with Lennon.

They feel that people who can't afford shoes should pull themselves up by their bootstraps.

Stupid Says . . .

66There is no housing shortage in Lincoln today—just
a rumour that is put about by people who have
nowhere to live.99

—Former mayor of Lincoln, England, G.L. Murfin

The Peabrain Politico Dictionary

Affirmative action: What happens when you
don't pay your taxes

Pundit: A pun bandit

Subcommittee: Underwater meetings

Politicus Ignoramous

The top ten signs that *you're* a dunderheaded
politician.

1. You cross your fingers every time you
   place your hand on a bible.
2. You spend twenty minutes answering a
   question and never actually answer the
   question.
3. You have no problem divulging top
   secret information to a reporter because
   Deep Throat got away with it.
4. You refer to your political enemies as
   "my very good friends" or "my esteemed
   colleagues."
5. You vote for going to war but deny that
   daddy got you out of military service.
6. Your salary as a public servant is $38,000
   a year, but your net worth is $2.5 million.
7. You can't pronounce "nuke-you-lure" or
   spell "potatoe."
8. You support tighter border restrictions,
   but none of your gardeners have green
   cards.
9. You've never passed a polygraph test.
10. You lobby to raise taxes, but get away
    with writing off "massage appointments"
    as medical deductions.

The Proverbial Politician

Balk softly and carry a big schtick.

Heels on Wheels

If politicians had cars named after them,
what would they be?

Al Sharpton: Honda Dissent

Dick Cheney: AMC Pacemaker

Queen Elizabeth: Dodge Coronation

Democratic Dimwits

Sure signs you're dealing with a
dunderheaded elected Democrat.

They think pornography is degrading to
women, except for the "art nouveau" films in
their private XXX collection.

They think the NRA supports a grammatical
error in the Constitution.

Snow Day

It was a cold winter morning when Bill Clinton took a walk on the White House lawn. Much to his dismay, he noticed that someone had whizzed in the snow to spell the word: "Philanderer." Furious, he immediately ordered the FBI and the CIA to launch an investigation as to who could've performed such a heinous act. After analyzing the situation and running lab tests an agent reported to Clinton in the Oval Office. "What did you find out?" Billy asked anxiously. The agent looked sheepish. "I've got bad news and . . . uh . . . worse news, sir." Clinton stood up, and asked to hear the bad news first. "Well, it appears that it was Al Gore who whizzed in the snow." Clinton gasped. "Y'all have got to be kidding me. What's the worse news?" The agent shook his head. "It was Hillary's handwriting."

Lost in Translation

WHAT YOU SAY:
Are you aware of all the acid rain?

WHAT A STUPID POLITICIAN HEARS:
Thank God all politicians are sane.

Film at Eleven

Favorite films of the truly daft.

Richard Nixon: *On the Watergate*

Mike Huckabee: *The Plying Game*

Newt Gingrich: *Love is a Many Splendored Fling*

Bumper Snickers!

I HAVE AN EXCELLENT MEMORY, IT'S
JUST VERY SHORT.
Mitt Romney

FOR EVERY ACTION THERE IS AN EQUAL
AND OPPOSITE GOVERNMENT PROGRAM.
Ralph Nader

Promises, Promises . . .

WHAT THE CANDIDATE PROMISES:
*To curtail the importation of foreign goods, thereby
creating more jobs for their constituents.*

WHAT THE ELECTED OFFICIAL DOES:
*Increases the importation of melamine-tainted pet
food and lead-based toys.*

Sex, Lies, and Videotape

You might think a Democratic "golden boy" from the staunchly Democratic state of West Virginia could get caught with his pants down and get away with it, particularly after Bill Clinton set the standard for charming one's way through an adultery scandal. For West Virginia's Bob Wise, the future looked pretty rosy as his political career took off soon after his 1975 graduation from Tulane University with a law degree. He buzzed through a seat in the state Senate and then moved on to serve in the U.S. Congress, where loyal and satisfied West Virginians re-elected him to seven more terms. Wise shifted gears to run as governor of the state, and West Virginians handed him the win on a platter in 2000, but three years later the married-with-children golden boy vastly overestimated his appeal after he got caught red-handed in a love affair with a married woman. Taking a page from the Clinton playbook, Wise poured on the hat-in-hand contrition act, but his popularity and support evaporated under blazing public backlash. Wise's only act of wisdom was to avoid running for a second term.

Open Mouth. Insert Foot.

Match the pinheaded politico with their bone-headed blather.

a. Charles De Gaulle

b. Wesley Bolin

c. Dan Quayle

d. Richard Nixon

e. Ted Kennedy

f. Marion Barry

g. Ronald Reagan

h. Dwight D. Eisenhower

i. Bob Dole

j. George Dubya Bush

1. "First, it was not a strip bar, it was an erotic club. And second, what can I say? I'm a night owl."

2. "Rarely is the question asked: Is our children learning?"

3. "China is a big country, inhabited by many Chinese."

4. "The Internet is a great way to get on the Net."

5. "The world is more like it is now that it ever has been before.

6. "I favor access to discrimination on the basis of sexual orientation."

7. "Facts are stupid things."

8. "It is wonderful to be here in the great state of Chicago."

9. "I'm not for women, frankly, in any job. I don't want any of them around. Thank God we don't have any in the Cabinet."

10. "We'd like to avoid problems, because when we have problems, we can have troubles."

Answers:
1-f, 2-j, 3-a,
4-i, 5-h, 6-
e, 7-g, 8-c,
9-d, 10-b

The Peabrain Politico Dictionary

Freedom of Information Act: The civil right to bury yourself in red tape

Misdemeanor: A mistress with attitude

Paradox: What uninsured citizens can't afford

Democratic Dimwits

Sure signs you're dealing with a dunderheaded elected Democrat.

They campaigned for Anita Hill, but insist that Bill Clinton doesn't have a cigar problem.

They still think that guns kill people.

Republican Numbnuts

Sure signs you're dealing with a harebrained elected Republican.

They claim there's no such thing as "dirty" air because it all looks clean to them.

They think Dubya is actually running the country.

Presidential Pinheads

It was January 2002, when Dubya was hanging around his White House bedroom watching the Baltimore Colts play the Miami Dolphins. Before he knew it, the Prez was on the floor, apparently having fainted and fallen off the couch. Was the incident brought on by NFL excitement or perhaps the thrill of successfully running the most powerful nation on the planet? Nope. The Commander-in-Chief choked on a pretzel and passed out. Imagine that. The biggest terrorist threat in the White House is Rold Gold. Dubya had a lot to show for his junk food encounter, including a bruised lower lip, a scrape, and a large bruise on the left cheekbone. Of course the irony of the pretzel incident is inescapable, considering Dubya is usually choking on his words.

HOW CAN YOU TELL IF A
POLITICIAN IS LYING?

THEIR LIPS
ARE MOVING.

Democracy Inaction

The term "Watergate" turned into a catch-all for the series of political scandals that destroyed Richard Nixon's administration, and ultimately his presidency. The sordid mess began when Nixon authorized a bizarre and paranoid campaign to spy on and sabotage Democratic presidential candidates. A team of Nixon conspirators broke in to "bug" the Democratic National Headquarters at the Watergate complex in Washington, D.C., and were soon arrested, triggering a cover-up by Nixon and his cohorts. Dogged investigations by *Washington Post* reporters Carl Bernstein and Bob Woodward, who developed an inside source known as "Deep Throat," produced evidence of slush funds for hush money, illegal wiretaps, more burglaries, political espionage, and campaign fraud—and Nixon was at the center of the firestorm. His final undoing came from his own White House tape recordings that revealed his complicity in the cover-up of the Watergate burglary and evidence that he'd obstructed legal investigations. It took a U.S. Supreme Court ruling to force Nixon to hand over the tapes, and with an impeachment, conviction, and a possible prison sentence on the horizon, Tricky Dick resigned from office.

Bumper Snickers!

REAL WOMEN DON'T HAVE HOT FLASHES—
THEY HAVE POWER SURGES.
Hillary Clinton

ONLY IN AMERICA CAN A VIETNAM VET
LIVE IN A CARDBOARD BOX AND A DRAFT
DODGER LIVE IN THE WHITE HOUSE.
Dennis Kucinich

Heels on Wheels

If politicians had cars named after them,
what would they be?

Patrick Kennedy: Chevy DUI Citation

Bob Livingston: Dodge Tramp

Robert Hanssen: Buick Doublecross

Lost in Translation

WHAT YOU SAY:
Did you have sexual relations with that woman?

WHAT A STUPID POLITICIAN HEARS:
*When it comes to public relations would
you hire a woman?*

Republican Numbnuts

Sure signs you're dealing with a harebrained
elected Republican.

They don't worry about getting busted for
having a mistress because the Almighty will
forgive them.

They think the mercury in fish makes it
taste better.

The Peabrain Politico Dictionary

Experience: The name politicians
give their mistakes

Fascist: A right wing extremist who dislikes
facial features

Political party: Six exotic dancers and a
case of Dom Perignon

Stupid Says . . .

66We cannot build enough prisons to solve this problem. And the idea that we can keep incarcerating
and keep incarcerating—pretty soon we're not
going to have a young African American male population in America. They're all going to be in prison
or dead. One of the two.99

—John Edwards

The Proverbial Politician

The road to office is paved with rude intentions.

Nitwits in the News

The corrupt regime of Philippine despot Ferdinand Marcos was rife with repression, excess, political chaos, and human rights violations topped off by Marcos bilking the government of billions of dollars during his two-decade reign. Frightening as the regime was, there was an even bigger terror in the political cauldron: Imelda Marcos. Known as "the steel butterfly," her obsessive penchant for jewels, art, clothes, and shoes was rivaled only by her talent for self-delusion and sense of entitlement. As the Philippines' first lady and special envoy, she reveled in her glory, once stating: "Filipinos want beauty. I have to look beautiful so that the poor Filipinos will have a star to look at from their slums," and "I get so tired listening to one million dollars here, one million dollars there, it's so petty." When Marcos was deposed in 1986 and the couple exiled to Hawaii, Imelda's extravagance was laid bare. In her closet were 1,060 pairs of shoes, fifteen mink coats, almost 900 purses, and over 500 evening gowns. "I was no Marie Antoinette," she said. "I was not born to nobility, but I had a right to nobility." *Oh puhleeze.*

Film at Eleven

Favorite films of the truly daft.

Gary Condit: *Raiders of the Last Park*

Monica Lewinsky: *27 GAP Dresses*

Rudy Giuliani: *Days of Whine and Posers*

Promises, Promises . . .

WHAT THE CANDIDATE PROMISES:
To switch motorists to hybrid vehicles in the hopes of saving the environment.

WHAT THE ELECTED OFFICIAL DOES:
Buys his family a fleet of Hummers and four-wheel drive SUVs.

WHAT'S THE WORST THING
ABOUT HEARING A
POLITICAL JOKE?

THEY GET ELECTED.

Lost in Translation

WHAT YOU SAY:
Because of you I lost my job and pension.

WHAT A STUPID POLITICIAN HEARS:
Thank you for the tax extension.

Promises, Promises . . .

WHAT THE CANDIDATE PROMISES:
To educate citizens about the sanctity of family togetherness.

WHAT THE ELECTED OFFICIAL DOES:
Knocks up his mistress and announces that his twelve-year-old son is in rehab.

Politicos in the Pokey

One of a handful of Navy flying aces to come out of the Vietnam War, Randy "Duke" Cunningham went on to become one of the most visible and controversial Congressmen to land in the hoosegow in recent history. Cunningham was elected in 1990, after hammering his opponent about sexual harassment allegations and vowing to be "a Congressman we can be proud of." Cunningham's world fell apart after defense contractor Mitchell Wade purchased Cunningham's Del Mar house for $1.6 million in 2003, and then sold it for what it was actually worth, which was $700,000 less. Cunningham's windfall profit triggered investigations that revealed a conspiracy to commit tax evasion, mail fraud, and bribery, and by the time Cunningham's improprieties were exposed, he was living in a $2.5 million mansion filled with antiques and owned a condo, a yacht, and a Rolls Royce. The Feds soon established that he'd accepted nearly $2.4 million in bribes and goods from three separate defense contractors who reaped the benefits of Cunningham's position on a defense appropriations committee. The disgraced Congressman resigned, accepted a plea deal, and is serving an eight-year prison sentence. Nice going, Ace.

The Peabrain Politico Dictionary

Megalopolis: The size of Dubya's ego

Foreign affairs: Swedish mistresses

Democracy: Randomly exported products to disinterested nations

Heels on Wheels

If politicians had cars named after them, what would they be?

Sandy Berger: Suzuki Shredder

Newt Gingrich: Dodge Grifter

J. Edgar Hoover: Dodge Sniper

The Proverbial Politician

It's always darkest before the recall.

Just Say *Duh*!

Accidents do happen, but when Vice President Dick Cheney shot Texas attorney Harry Whittington on February 11, 2006, during a quail hunt in Texas, accounts of the situation flew like, well . . . like birdshot. In the aftermath of the debacle, it wasn't the accident we found amusing so much as some of the comments made by people surrounding the incident. Kenedy County Sheriff Ramon Salinas who investigated the scene noted that these things occur "not frequently, but often." Is that like not often, but frequently? Katharine Armstrong, who owns the land Cheney's group was hunting on, noted that: "The nature of quail shooting ensures that this will happen. It goes with the turf." You get the impression quail hunters are stumbling into a war zone every time they go into the field. Whittington survived the ordeal after spending six days in the hospital, and graciously said: "My family and I are deeply sorry for everything Vice President Cheney and his family have had to deal with." It's not often a gunshot victim actually apologizes to his attacker—accident or not.

Job Security

It was show and tell for little Billy's fourth grade class and the topic of the day was sharing with everyone what each child's father does for a living. The teacher asked one little girl about her father, and she proudly said that he's a fireman. Another girl said her father was an accountant. Another boy said his was a driving instructor. Then the teacher asked Billy what profession his father practiced. Billy eagerly answered. "He's an exotic dancer," he said. "Every night he takes his clothes off for strange men and on Thursdays he does private parties." The room went silent and Billy's shocked teacher pulled him aside after sending everyone out for recess. "Billy, is what you said about your father really true?" Billy shook his head. "Nah," he whispered. "He really works for the Bush Administration. I was too embarrassed to let the other kids know."

Government Bondage

The top ten things that identify you as a government employee.

1. The first thing you hear from your supervisor every morning is "when you have some free time."
2. You stop asking questions because you know that no one will actually have an answer.
3. You're thrilled with a pay raise of one percent.
4. Your office is filled with Dilbert cartoons.
5. You've been sitting at the same desk for five years, have five different business cards, and your nameplate is taped to your cubicle wall.
6. Your title is: "Computer Tech, Grade Two."
7. You never discuss work, so your family assumes you work for the CIA.
8. Every project you're given is already two months late the day it's assigned to you.
9. You send out your resume twice a month.
10. You're constantly attending conferences that have nothing to do with your job.

The Proverbial Politician

Early to mislead, good with the lies, makes a politician wealthy and quick to deny.

Bumper Snickers!

IF YOU DON'T LIKE THE WAY WE COUNT VOTES IN FLORIDA, THEN TAKE I-95 AND VISIT ONE OF THE OTHER FIFTY-SIX STATES.
Katherine Harris

DOES THE NAME PAVLOV RING A BELL?
George Bush

Just Say *Duh*!

After schlepping through over three decades worth of crappy movies from *Hercules in New York* to *Conan the Barbarian* to *Collateral Damage*, few of us would've guessed that the Terminator would one day become the Governator. But run for office he did, and now Arnold Schwarzenegger is running the state of California. His journey toward winning his election, however, took a bit of finagling and more than a few true lies, when in 2003 a half-dozen women accused Arnie of groping and sexual harassment. Lacking total recall of the incidents at first, Arnie finally conceded that he had indeed "behaved badly" in his youth and blathered out a general apology to everyone he'd ever offended. Chief among his accusers was Anna Richardson, a British television host, who actually sued the up-and-coming political predator for grabbing her hooter on-camera in 2000. Unfortunately for Arnie, that incident was recorded, despite his attempts to downplay his grievous grope. Inexperienced spin doctors would've signaled the end of days for Arnie, but luckily for him the matter was settled out of court. Dare we say, he managed to *eraser*?

Democratic Dimwits

Sure signs you're dealing with a dunderheaded
elected Democrat.

They insist that the purpose of "real government" is to protect the "little guy."

Whenever they hear the word Chappaquiddick, they get defensive and insist Ted Kennedy wasn't driving.

Film at Eleven

Favorite films of the truly daft.

J. Edgar Hoover: *The Taste of Wrath*
Condoleezza Rice: *Executive Indecision*
Janet Reno: *Bowling for Colombians*

When Hell Freezes Over

It's a slow day in heaven, when St. Peter hears a knock on the Pearly Gates. "Who goes there?" he asks. "It's me. Bill Clinton. Two-time American president." St. Peter rolls his eyes. "Enter." The gates slowly open and, sure enough, Clinton walks through. "So tell me, Mr. Clinton. What terrible things did you do when you were alive?" Clinton thinks for a second. "Well, Almighty, I smoked a bit of dope, but I never inhaled. And I had this thing with an intern and a cigar, but I never actually cheated on my wife." St. Peter scowls. "Anything else?" Clinton nods sorrowfully. "Actually, I lied on many occasions, but I didn't actually commit perjury. So do I get to go to heaven?" St. Peter thinks for a moment. "Tell you what. I'm going to send you to a very hot place, but we won't call it 'hell.' You'll be there for a very long time, but we won't call it 'eternity,'" St. Peter grins. "Oh, and don't abandon all hope when you get there—just don't hold your breath waiting for it to freeze over."

Democracy Inaction

When President George Bush nominated Clarence Thomas to replace the retiring Thurgood Marshall on the Supreme Court bench in 1991, confirmation appeared to be a foregone conclusion—until University of Oklahoma law school professor Anita Hill appeared before the Senate Judiciary Committee with shocking allegations. Hill had worked as an assistant for Thomas at the Equal Employment Opportunity Commission where, according to Hill's testimony, Thomas graphically discussed pornographic films and actors, and boasted about his own sexual expertise. In one well publicized comment, Hill testified that Thomas had been drinking soda out of a can, and at one point looked at it and said: "Who has put pubic hair on my Coke?" Hill's testimony was followed by similar statements from other former assistants of Thomas. After debating the issue, the Senate Judiciary Committee passed his nomination on to a full Senate vote without a recommendation either way. Thomas was confirmed by a vote of fifty-two to forty-eight, the narrowest margin in a century. Ain't it comforting to know who's making decisions for you?

The Peabrain Politico Dictionary

Congress: An exclusive club with a $30 million initiation fee

Ballot: *The Nutcracker Suite*

Interventionism: Going to rehab

Stupid Says . . .

66 I even accept for the sake of argument that sexual orgies eliminate social tensions and ought to be encouraged. 99

—Supreme Court Justice Antonin Scalia

Republican Numbnuts

Sure signs you're dealing with a harebrained elected Republican.

The only news they believe is what's being reported on FOX.

They think Birkenstock was a hippie rock concert that took place in the 1960s.

WHY DID GOD GIVE POLITICIANS ONE MORE BRAIN CELL THAN HORSES?

SO THEY WOULDN'T CRAP IN FRONT OF THE PODIUM.

Sex, Lies, and Videotape

A vice bust in Florida turned into political theater when Bob Allen, a member of the Florida House of Representatives, was tagged for soliciting a male undercover cop for oral sex in a public restroom on July 11, 2007. Just months before his arrest, Allen co-sponsored a bill to increase the penalty of public sex charges from a misdemeanor to a felony. Officer Danny Kavanaugh and two other officers were working a burglary detail when Allen came to the Veterans Memorial Park in Titusville, Florida. Suspecting Allen was looking for a little mischief, Kavanaugh went into a restroom and entered the handicapped stall. According to Kavanaugh, Allen followed him into the stall and offered $20 to perform oral sex. Allen's lawyer came up with amusing rationalizations for his client, including the allegation that the reason Allen suggested sex was that he was fearful for his life. Well, sure. Doesn't everybody go around offering scary people sex for twenty bucks? The debacle forced Allen to resign his political office after being convicted of a second-degree misdemeanor. Luckily for Allen, his bill that could have made this a full-blown felony failed to pass.

Lost in Translation

WHAT YOU SAY:
Because of you we're all in hell.

WHAT A STUPID POLITICIAN HEARS:
Because of you our lives are swell.

Democratic Dimwits

Sure signs you're dealing with a dunderheaded elected Democrat.

They think that Ayn Rand is South African currency.

They think Supply Side Economics refers to the Colombian drug cartels.

Politicos in the Pokey

In 1978, the FBI launched a sting operation, dubbed Abscam, to target trafficking in stolen property, but ultimately to investigate legislative malfeasance by setting up the fictitious "Abdul Enterprises, Ltd." Posing agents as Middle East businessmen, over three dozen U.S. congressmen and senators were approached with offers of bribes. Seven took the bait, including one senator and six congressmen. New Jersey Senator Harrison Williams, and congressmen John Jenrette of South Carolina, Michael Myers and Raymond Lederer of Pennsylvania, Frank Thompson of New Jersey, John Murphy of New York, and Richard Kelly of Florida, were tried separately on conspiracy and bribery charges in 1981. Five other government officials at the state and local levels also walked into the trap. In the aftermath of Abscam, close scrutiny and fallout fell, not on Congress or the Senate, but on the FBI because of serious allegations of entrapment that in one case led to the overturning of a conviction, although it was later reinstated by a higher court. Since Abscam, the FBI has curtailed legislative sting operations, apparently preferring to bust crooks after they commit crimes on their own.

Mistaken Identity

A congressman and his driver were speeding through the rural countryside en route to the airport, when all of a sudden a pig ran across the road. The driver swerved to miss the bovine, but to no avail. Piggy went splat! Spying a farmhouse in the distance, the driver pulled up to the house and knocked on the door. The congressman watched as the driver entered the house, only to emerge fifteen minutes later with a bottle of whiskey, smoking a Cuban cigar, and carry a huge box of $100 bills. As the driver got into the car, the congressman was astounded. "Wow. What did you tell those folks?" The driver chuckled. "Nothing much. I simply explained that I was the driver for their congressman, and that I'd killed the pig."

The Peabrain Politico Dictionary

Capitalism: A rebellion against
lowercase letters

Think tank: The Pentagon's septic system

Pocket veto: Deciding to keep
Slick Willy zipped up

Lost in Translation

WHAT YOU SAY:
Every world leader hates you.

WHAT A STUPID POLITICIAN HEARS:
You're so smart that nothing escapes you.

The Know-It-All Award for Unprecedented Obscurity

Every politician has had rhetorical gaffes during their tenure on Capitol Hill. Dan Quayle was a nightmare, and Dubya is the undisputed king of verbal carnage. But in this instance, we pay homage to former Secretary of Defense Donald Rumsfeld, whose terminally obtuse statements put everyone into a coma. His most unbearable utterance occurred on February 12, 2002, during a Department of Defense news briefing. The question put to Rummy was simple: "In regard to Iraq weapons of mass destruction and terrorists, is there any evidence to indicate that Iraq has attempted to or is willing to supply terrorists with weapons of mass destruction?" His answer: "Reports that say that something hasn't happened are always interesting to me, because as we know, there are known knowns; there are things we know we know. We also know there are known unknowns; that is to say we know there are some things we do not know. But there are also unknown unknowns—the ones we don't know we don't know. And if one looks throughout the history of our country and other free countries, it is the latter category that tend to be the difficult ones."

Democratic Dimwits

Sure signs you're dealing with a dunderheaded elected Democrat.

They get goosebumps listening to Barbra Streisand sing "The Way We Were."

They think low income housing is a great idea—as long as it's not in *their* neighborhood.

The Peabrain Politico Dictionary

Political correctness: An unknown entity

Filibuster: A horse whisperer

Statutory law: The protection of monuments

Lost in Translation

WHAT YOU SAY:
You're the worst president we've ever had.

WHAT A STUPID POLITICIAN HEARS:
You're even better than your dad!

Presidential Pinheads

If it's any solace to the American public, our fearless leader isn't the only major political leader who screws up. On July 21, 2007, Yves Leterme, leader of the Flemish Christian Democrat party and front-runner for the position of Belgium's prime minister, did all but commit political suicide when he sang the wrong national anthem. The melodic blunder was made all the worse by the fact that it was Belgium's national day, and instead of singing *La Brabançonne*, Leterme began belting out the French national anthem, *La Marseillaise*. Given that Belgium is a country divided by its French and Flemish citizens, it was a huge oops. Could it have been any worse? Yep. When asked why Belgium held the celebration on July 21, Leterme gave the wrong answer. If they really wanted to go for the trifecta, they should've asked him the origin of Brussels sprouts.

The Proverbial Politician

There are only two things certain in life—
wealth and bilking taxes.

Film at Eleven

Favorite films of the truly daft.

George Bush: *Thank God it's Fry Day*

Bruce Babbit: *The Liar in Winter*

Vladimir Putin: *How the West Was Stunned*

The Peabrain Politico Dictionary

Division of labor: Making women
do all the work

Secret Service: Meeting a stripper named
Trixie at a cheap hotel

Theocracy: A group of Roosevelt extremists

Film at Eleven

Favorite films of the truly daft.

Lyndon Johnson: *Captains Outrageous*

Arnold Schwarzenegger: *Das Heel*

Bob Packwood: *Memoirs of a Douchebag*

The Proverbial Politician

The morass is always meaner for the other
side of the dense.

Nitwits in the News

Located in Northern Oregon, Arlington is a sleepy little town that over 500 citizens call home, and until January of 2008, most Oregonians probably couldn't point to it on a map. But they can now, courtesy of Arlington's mayor, Carmen Kontur-Gronquist, who thought nothing of posting her scantily clad big bad self on her MySpace page. In a town where you can practically toss a football from one end to the other, the scandal literally put Arlington on the map when it hit national news. Of course it didn't help that Kontur-Gronquist, provocatively posed in a black bra and panties, was standing in front of one of the city's rural protection fire trucks. Did we mention that she's also the fire department's executive secretary? *Oops!* The lingerie lovin' mayor claims her personal life has "nothing to do with my mayor's position." Indeed, she says she's not going to change and people need to "get over it." Many of her constituents disagree and are calling for her resignation. Others defend her right to flaunt her stuff, citing the real reason for the grudge is a dispute over a public golf course. Gives new meaning to foreplay, eh?

Stupid Says . . .

"They don't call me Tyrannosaurus Sex for nothing.**"**

—Ted Kennedy while dressed as Barney for an office Christmas party

Democratic Dimwits

Sure signs you're dealing with a dunderheaded elected Democrat.

They feel guilty for laughing at dumb blonde jokes.

They still don't get why everyone is so hard on Jane Fonda.

Lip Service

It was the 1988 Republican National Convention when George Bush uttered an astonishing line of bull that we wouldn't believe if our own mothers said it: "Congress will push me to raise taxes and I'll say no. And they'll push, and I'll say no, and they'll push again, and I'll say, to them, 'Read my lips: no new taxes.'" Yeah, *right.* Ten thousand tax hikes later, we're still paying for his rhetoric, say nothing of the sins of his progeny. Read a few of Papa Bush's gaffes and you'll see it's genetic:

"It's no exaggeration to say that the undecideds could go one way or another."

"For seven and a half years I've worked alongside President Reagan. We've had triumphs. Made some mistakes. We've had some sex . . . uh . . . setbacks."

"Boy, they were big on crematoriums, weren't they?"

—During a 1989 tour of Auschwitz

"I put confidence in the American people, in their ability to sort through what is fair and what is unfair, what is ugly and what is unugly."

"I have opinions of my own, strong opinions, but I don't always agree with them."

Nitwits in the News

If you knew the King of England was coming to your place for dinner, what would you serve? Lobster? Filet Mignon? Oysters Rockefeller? Hot dogs? With the all-important decision being made by Eleanor Roosevelt, she chose the latter. Yes, it's true. It was June 1939 when England's King George VI and Queen Elizabeth paid a visit to FDR and the First Lady. And a truly historic meeting it was, marking the first time a reigning British Monarch set foot in America. And what did the Royals get for their trouble? Tubes of death with mustard. To be fair, hot dogs are as American as apple pie and a staple at picnics, which Eleanor and her husband hosted for the royals at their Hyde Park estate. And in a thank you letter to Eleanor, Elizabeth did mention that their children loved the hot dogs. But FDR's mother was reportedly horrified that the Brits were made to eat the tubers while sitting on the porch of the Roosevelt's cottage. Many felt it was the ultimate First Lady faux pas, but when you think about it, it could've been much worse. Eleanor could've served SPAM.

The Peabrain Politico Dictionary

Conservatives: Ex-prisoners who make jam

Lame duck politics: Dick Cheney on
a hunting trip

Banana Republic: A Dole conspiracy

Just Say *Duh*!

If you think American taxpayers are the only folks getting taken to the cleaners by their government, guess again. In the Romanian town of Giurgiu, Mayor Lucian Iliescu takes special care of his female employees during the International Women's Day celebration. On March 8, 2006, Iliescu spent public funds on a party for 350 people, providing flowers to each female guest and a "show of professional artists." At a cost of around $14,000 to taxpayers, the party went as planned. What cost so much, you ask? Well it wasn't flowers. Iliescu's "professional artists" were male strippers.

Stupid Says . . .

❝do not like this word 'bomb.' It is not a bomb. It is a device that is exploding.❞

—Jacques le Blanc, former French ambassador to New Zealand, commenting on nuclear weapons

Heels on Wheels

If politicians had cars named after them, what would they be?

Donald Lukens: Pontiac Bribe

Betty Ford: Mini Stupor

Dennis Kucinich: Chrysler Pacifist

Read 'Em and Weep

Political tomes that never made the bestseller list.

1. *How Hooked on Phonics Changed My Life* by Dan Quayle
2. *Shoot First and Ask Questions Later* by Dick Cheney
3. *I Married a Putz* by Hillary Clinton
4. *Bambi: A Stripper's Tale* by Ted Kennedy
5. *How I Invented the Internet and Saved the World from Melting* by Al Gore
6. *Weapons of Bass Destruction: The Ultimate Fishing Guide* by George "Dubya" Bush
7. *How to Save $400 a Day by Cutting Your Own Hair* by John Edwards
8. *Closing the GAP: An Intern's Guide to Sex, Scandal, and Stogies* by Monica Lewinsky
9. *I Know What I Know and I Want You to Know What I Know* by Donald Rumsfeld
10. *Feminism. Ain't it Cute?* by Rush Limbaugh

Republican Numbnuts

Sure signs you're dealing with a harebrained elected Republican.

They believe that Jesus was a blond, blue-eyed white guy.

They think Ann Coulter is hot *and* brilliant.

Promises, Promises . . .

WHAT THE CANDIDATE PROMISES:
To crack down on vice and illegal gambling.

WHAT THE ELECTED OFFICIAL DOES:
Picks up a hooker and drops $5,000 on the Colts.

Democratic Dimwits

Sure signs you're dealing with a dunderheaded elected Democrat.

They think the flat tax rate is a good idea—as long as it's 90 percent.

They think that same sex marriage should be ratified, but nativity scenes made illegal.

Heels on Wheels

If politicians had cars named after them, what would they be?

Bob Allen: Ford Escort Service

Monica Lewinsky: Dodge Foreplay

John Edwards: Chevy Maliboob

The Potty Cruising Cretin Award

A plainclothes cop investigating illicit activity in a restroom at the Minneapolis-St. Paul International Airport on June 11, 2007, arrested Senator Larry Craig of Idaho after the senator entered a stall next to the officer, tapped his foot, then slid his foot over to tap the officer's foot, and then waved his hand under the stall divider, all of which are considered gay cruising signals indicating interest in a sexual encounter. The officer was more interested in making an arrest. Craig took the unorthodox approach of pleading guilty to a misdemeanor by signing and mailing a plea agreement on August 1, 2007, apparently hoping no one would pay much attention. No such luck. The story broke on August 27, and Craig cried entrapment, blustering that the cop had misconstrued an "innocent" foot bump, that Craig had been waving his hand around under the divider simply to retrieve a piece of paper, and that he'd pled guilty only to avoid a public trial. Well, the *last* part is probably true. Craig continues tap dancing around the pressure to resign, and the bathroom stall has become a major attraction. Way to increase tourism!

Lost in Translation

WHAT YOU SAY:
You stole all that charity money.

WHAT A STUPID POLITICIAN HEARS:
Who knew that you were so funny?

Film at Eleven

Favorite films of the truly daft.

Barbara Bush: *Jurassic Snark*

John Kerry: *Lie Another Day*

Ken Calvert: *One Flew Over the Hooker's Breast*

Presidential Pinheads

One would think that as president of the world's most powerful nation, a person would develop the ability to let sniping and criticism roll off one's back. Not so for Harry S. Truman—especially when it came at his daughter's expense. In 1950, after a concert where Margaret Truman performed, *Washington Post* critic Paul Hume wrote that Margaret had a "pleasant voice of little size and fair quality" and asserted that she "cannot sing very well," is "flat a good deal of the time," and "cannot sing anything approaching professional finish." Harry didn't take that well. In a letter to Hume, Truman exclaimed: "Some day I hope to meet you. When that happens you'll need a new nose, a lot of beefsteak for black eyes, and perhaps a supporter below!" To his credit, Papa Truman did what any father would likely have done; however, as president he perhaps could've issued his retribution simply by having J. Edgar Hoover send a couple of undercover FBI agents over to break Hume's legs.

The Proverbial Politician

An ounce of intervention is worth a pound of obscure.

Lost in Translation

WHAT YOU SAY:
Your vice president shot a man.

WHAT A STUPID POLITICIAN HEARS:
Your vice president is a stouthearted man.

Mix and Mingle: Presidential Pinhead Anagrams

a. Millard Fillmore

b. George Bush

c. Franklin Pierce

d. Bill Clinton

e. Richard Nixon

f. Grover Cleveland

g. Herbert Hoover

h. Ronald Reagan

i. Martin Van Buren

j. Gerald Ford

1. CLANGED REVOLVER

2. ADRENAL GROAN

3. LARDED FROG

4. BROTHER EVEROH

5. BUGGER SHOE

6. INFERNAL PICKER

7. NIL LINTBLOC

8. RANCID XIHORN

9. MAIMED ROLLFRILL

10. VARMINT BEANRUN

Answers:
1-f, 2-h, 3-j,
4-g, 5-b, 6-
c, 7-d, 8-e,
9-a, 10-i

The Proverbial Politician

Good fences make good profits.

Democratic Dimwits

Sure signs you're dealing with a dunderheaded elected Democrat.

In their office they maintain a shrine to John Lennon.

They argue that poverty can be eliminated with broader government-based programs and redistribution of middle-class wealth.

The Peabrain Politico Dictionary

Crony capitalism: The U.S. Senate

Recession: What Congressmen fear most about their hairlines

Checkbook diplomacy: Withdrawing funds from campaign donations

Live Long and Prosper

When a congressman and his wife married he put a lock box in their closet and made her promise she would never peek. She agreed, and for the next three decades she never opened it. But on their thirtieth wedding anniversary, she could no longer contain her curiosity and opened the box, which contained six empty Budweiser cans and $84,484 in cash. She was shocked by the money, but was baffled by the cans. That night at dinner she confessed her transgression. "All these years I've kept the promise and never looked in the box," she began. "But today, I just couldn't help it. I had to look. Could you tell me why you saved the beer cans?" The congressman thought for a second. "Well, it's like this. Whenever I cheated on you I put an empty can in the box as a reminder to never do it again." His wife was shocked, but decided to forgive him. "But dear, why so much cash?" she asked. "Well, whenever the box was overflowing with empty cans, I took them to the recycling center and redeemed them for cash."

Democracy Inaction

For most of us, a bounced check usually results in a plethora of bank fees and penalties that far exceed the amount of the check. Not so for Congressmen in 1992, when the House Banking scandal broke wide open, infuriating the public and helping to upset the balance of power in Congress. As far as scandals go, the House Banking Scandal wasn't that big a deal, but it did highlight the reality that members of the ruling classes often get to play by very different rules than us mere mortals. The House Bank acted as a sort of clearinghouse where Congressmen could cash their paychecks. If they needed a little extra cash, the House Bank was also a place where they could overdraw their accounts free of charge for as much as the amount of their next paycheck—and pay it back whenever they wanted. Over 355 of 435 Congressional members took advantage of the penalty-free perk, and several were indicted after an investigation showed more serious indiscretions linked to House Banking practices. At least the embarrassment put the kibosh on Congressmen laughing all the way to the bank.

Republican Numbnuts

Sure signs you're dealing with a harebrained elected Republican.

They fully support the war given what that evil Saddam did to Dubya's daddy.

After a lobotomy their intelligence quotient goes up fifty points.

Promises, Promises . . .

WHAT THE CANDIDATE PROMISES:
To prosecute factories responsible for polluting oceans and waterways.

WHAT THE ELECTED OFFICIAL DOES:
Eliminates restrictions on off-shore drilling and outlaws dolphin-safe tuna.

Nitwits in the News

During a radio interview in June 1998 with conservative host Armstrong Williams, Senate Majority Leader Trent Lott managed to insult every gay person on the planet when asked if he considered homosexuality a sin. Lott replied: "Yes it is," and then continued with a bizarre diatribe that equated homosexuality with alcoholism and—of all things—kleptomania. Lott went on to suggest that the "cure" for homosexuality was the same as the cures for any other addiction. Bill Clinton's press secretary, Mike McCurry, remarked that Lott's extremist commentary "is an indicator of how difficult it is to do rational work in Washington." No kidding. Lott stuck his foot in his mouth again on December 5, 2002, at a birthday party for infamous racist and segregationist Senator Strom Thurmond when he said: "When Strom Thurmond ran for president, we voted for him. We're proud of it. And if the rest of the country had followed our lead, we wouldn't have had all these problems over the years either." Lott's idiotic comments triggered a firestorm of outrage, and two weeks later he resigned his position as majority leader. As well he should have. Moron.

WHY DID THE POLITICIAN
CROSS THE
R O A D ?

TO MAKE SURE THE CHICKEN
PAID ITS TAXES.

The Proverbial Politician

Votes only count in snafus and hanging chads.

The Peabrain Politico Dictionary

Caucus: The capital of New Jersey

Lobbyist: A foyer inspector

Staying the course: Making the same stupid mistakes over and over and over

Heels on Wheels

If politicians had cars named after them, what would they be?

John McCain: Ford Unfocused

Hillary Clinton: Dodge Political Dynasty

Bob Packwood: Chevy Luv Affair

Sex, Lies, and Videotape

Creepy Congressmen abound in Washington, but few reach the level of Floridian Mark Foley's scuzzbag behavior. The sordid details began surfacing in September 2006, revealing that Foley had been trading sexually explicit e-mails and text messages with teenage boys who'd served as congressional pages. One page was just sixteen when Foley began pestering him with e-mails that the young man described as "sick." Another page, who was seventeen, was offered a stay at the congressman's home for oral sex, and yet another received an e-mail from Foley requesting a sexually graphic photograph. Part of the horror of Foley's perversion is that his activities and sexual orientation were well known and largely ignored in Congress for years. Another hair-raising irony in Foley's behavior is that he authored a reform package that included stringent penalties for online predators who target children, and worked closely with child protection advocates. Under intense fire from Congressional leaders, Foley signed a letter of resignation just one day after the story went public and left Congress in utter disgrace. We're still hoping for news that the slimeball will face criminal charges.

What's Your Sign?

The top ten pick-up lines that work on Bill Clinton.

1. I'm Mindy. Are you looking for a new intern?
2. Is that a stain on my dress, or are you just happy to see me?
3. Would you like to help the homeless and take me home with you?
4. My name is "Milk" and I'll do your body good.
5. I'd love to see your hanging chads.
6. I'm choking. I need mouth to mouth!
7. Have you ever played "Spank the Constituent?"
8. I'm a freelance proctologist. When was your last checkup?
9. If I was Russia would you invade me?
10. Cigar?

Just Say *Duh*!

Currently serving his fourth term as mayor of Boston, Thomas Menino has done plenty for Bean Town. Unfortunately, he doesn't always have a way with words. When discussing the shortage of parking in his fair city he asserted that: "It's like an Alcatraz around my neck." And then there was the time he described former Boston Mayor John Collins, saying "He was a man of great statue." Is there something in the politician's handbook that says once you become a mucky muck your rhetorical skills drop to that of an eggplant?

The Peabrain Politico Dictionary

Amendment: Tacking a bad idea onto a worse one

Gross National Product: A boatload of fake vomit

Bureaucrat: A guy who builds dressers

The Proverbial Politician

Voters can't be choosers.

Bumper Snickers!

LEAVE NO BILLIONAIRES BEHIND!
Bush/Cheney in 2004

DON'T BLAME ME, I VOTED WITH THE
MAJORITY.
John Kerry

Promises, Promises . . .

WHAT THE CANDIDATE PROMISES:
To increase the oversight and prosecution of governmental misconduct.

WHAT THE ELECTED OFFICIAL DOES:
Moves his bribes into hidden offshore accounts.

Stupid Says . . .

"Give Bill a second term, and Al Gore and I will be turned loose to do what we really want to do."

—Hillary Clinton at a Democratic fundraiser

Nitwits in the News

It's no mystery that when the American public elected Dubya, it opened a Pandora's box of verbal gaffes the likes of which none of us could ever have imagined. Time and time again, the Texan Boy Blunder opens his mouth and issues statements that make Americans look like Hooked on Phonics dropouts. One of the more unforgivable statements came in May 2007, when Dubya hosted a formal state visit by Queen Elizabeth and her husband Prince Philip, a well-known gaffer himself. During his welcome speech to Liz, Dubya discussed her enduring history with ten American presidents, and then went on to say that: "You've helped our nation celebrate its bicentennial in 17 . . . in 1976." After aging the Queen by two centuries, Dubya then did the unthinkable and winked at her. Bad idea. Liz issued what Bush described as "a look that only a mother could give a child." Some days you step in it . . . some days you drown in it. On this day, Dubya sunk faster than a tyrannosaurus in the La Brea Tar Pits.

One Quayle Is Worth Two
in the Bush

For years, former Veep Dan Quayle held the title of world's most grammatically and geographically challenged politician. From his infamous "potatoe" debacle to his saying how wonderful it was to be "in the great state of Chicago," we still haven't forgotten the idiot who thinks America has forty-nine states.

66What a waste it is to lose one's mind. Or not to have a mind is being very wasteful. How true that is.99

66The Holocaust was an obscene period in our nation's history. I mean in this century's history. But we all lived in this century. I didn't live in this century.99

66When I have been asked during these last weeks who caused the riots and the killing in LA., my answer has been direct and simple: Who is to blame for the riots? The rioters are to blame. Who is to blame for the killings? The killers are to blame.99

66It's time for the human race to enter the solar system.99

—Commenting on the idea of sending a
manned mission to Mars

66Verbosity leads to unclear, inarticulate things.99

Bumper Snickers!

DON'T BE SEXIST—BITCHES HATE THAT.
Pat Robertson

NEVER UNDERESTIMATE THE POWER OF STUPID PEOPLE IN LARGE GROUPS.
The entire United States Congress

Republican Numbnuts

Sure signs you're dealing with a harebrained elected Republican.

They think WWII actually started at Pearl Harbor.

They think their C-plus grade average qualifies them to run for the presidency.

Presidential Pinheads

Pedro Miguel de Santana Lopes had a very short and tumultuous turn as Portugal's Prime Minister from 2004 to 2005, but politics aside, it was a host of bizarre and moronic blunders that made him an unsuccessful diplomat. For example, it's said that Lopes once called a press conference to discuss a threat that was made on his life. It seems he'd received the ominous warning in the mail and it read: *Cuidado com os rapazes*, or "Watch out for the boys." Lopes took it as a threat, but in reality it was just a piece of junk mail promoting a new book. Then there was the time he spoke of his favorite Chopin classical music pieces. Only trouble is, they were non-existent violin concertos. And as if that weren't enough, Lopes once had his secretary send a postcard to renowned Brazilian novelist and poet Machado de Assis. This too was a conundrum, given that Assis died in 1908. And you thought *we* had leadership issues?

Mix and Mingle: First Lady Anagrams

a. Mamie Eisenhower

b. Hillary Clinton

c. Pat Nixon

d. Lady Bird Johnson

e. Mary Todd Lincoln

f. Jackie Kennedy

g. Laura Bush

h. Nancy Reagan

i. Bess Truman

j. Dolly Madison

1. HULA BURSA

2. DOILY ALMONDS

3. CANNERY NAAG

4. ANTHILL CORNILY

5. NUMB STARES

6. SEAMIER HOMEWINE

7. DICKY KEENJEAN

8. BRANDY JOINHOLDS

9. NAP TOXIN

10. DYNAMIC TORNDOLL

Answers:
1-g, 2-j, 3-
h, 4-b, 5-i,
6-a, 7-f, 8-
d, 9-c, 10-e

Away in the Manger

After much debate, scandal, and billions of dollars spent on an investigative committee, it was finally decided that displaying a nativity scene anywhere in Washington, D.C., was a federal offense and would be prosecuted to the fullest extent of the law. Oddly enough, it wasn't a decision made due to religious convictions or constitutional rights. What finally sealed the deal was the simple fact that three wise men and a virgin couldn't be found anywhere in D.C. There was, however, no shortage of asses to fill a stable.

Democratic Dimwits

Sure signs you're dealing with a dunderheaded
elected Democrat.

They consider Al Gore the poster child for
global warming.

They think dealing with Bush means hiring
an illegal gardener.

The Proverbial Politician

If you're not imparting pollution, you're
not part of the fiefdom.

Just Say *Duh*!

Many politicians make really bad decisions and
still manage to stay in office. Others are not so lucky.
Take the case of former Oregon politician Jim Bunn.
Beginning in 1987 he served as Republican state
senator and in 1994, at the age of thirty-eight, was
elected to Congress. Shortly thereafter, it all went

to hell. After seventeen years of marriage and five kids, Bunn dumped his wife and wed staffer Sonja Skurdal. That move alone was wasn't enough to get everyone's knickers in a twist, but when he suddenly made Skurdal his chief of staff and put her on the Oregon state payroll for a whopping $97,000, heads began to roll. The bonehead move cost Bunn the 1996 election as he lost to Democrat Darlene Hooley. *Duh!* So what's Bunn up to now? He's making thirty grand a year as a swing shift prison guard at the Yamhill County jail in McMinnville, Oregon. Karma's a bitch.

Heels on Wheels

If politicians had cars named after them,
what would they be?

Donald Rumsfeld: Chevy Cavalier Attitude

Barack Obama: Mitsubishi Aspiration

Robert Novak: Volkswagon Blabber

Republican Numbnuts

Sure signs you're dealing with a harebrained elected Republican.

They have billions in mysterious tax-free income.

They erect shrines to Sean Hannity.

Lost in Translation

WHAT YOU SAY:
You're a no good draft dodger.

WHAT A STUPID POLITICIAN HEARS:
That John McCain is a jolly old codger!

The Proverbial Politician

If God meant for politicians to lie, he would've given them flings.

Presidential Pinheads

In yet another show of his own brand of presidential stupidity, George Dubya created one hell of a mess in December 2007 when he botched a hotline number during a nationally televised address about the mortgage crisis. Not known for his verbal accuracy or teleprompter competence, Dubya informed avid listeners to call a phone number for help with their mortgages. Trouble is, he gave the wrong number—not once, but twice. "I have a message for every homeowner worried about rising mortgages," Dubya said confidently, going on to say that the best thing we could do for our families was call 1-800-995-HOPE. Then he repeated it and the nation began dialing. Did anyone get help? Nope. The real number was 1-888-995-HOPE. Who did everyone get when they dialed Dubya's number? The Freedom Christian Academy in Texas. Coincidence? We think not.

Mr. Ed's Revenge

A guy walks into a cowboy bar and orders a drink just as Bill O'Reilly starts his monologue. The beer swilling guy listens for a minute and loudly proclaims: "That guy's the biggest horse's ass I've ever seen." Upon hearing the comment, a patron at the end of the bar approaches him and pops him one in the jaw as everyone in the bar applauds. Repositioning himself on his stool, the guy orders another beer, which the bartender sets in front of him. "Geez, man. This must be Bush country," he says to the bartender. "Nope," says the barkeep. "It's horse country."

You're *Not* the Boss of Me!

Isn't it amazing what a difference six months can make in the life of a stupid politician?

"The most important thing is for us to find Osama bin Laden. It is our number one priority and we will not rest until we find him."

—George Dubya Bush, September 13, 2001

"I don't know where bin Laden is. I have no idea and really don't care. It's not that important. It's not our priority."

—George Dubya Bush, March 13, 2002

Republican Numbnuts

Sure signs you're dealing with a harebrained elected Republican.

They can't pronounce "nuclear."

They think we could've won Vietnam if we'd have stayed a few more years.

Bumper Snickers!

> IF YOU HAVE TO CHOOSE BETWEEN THE
> LESSER OF THREE EVILS, PICK THE ONE
> YOU'VE NEVER VOTED FOR BEFORE.
> Ralph Nader

> LEAD ME NOT INTO TEMPTATION. I CAN
> FIND THE WAY MYSELF.
> Newt Gingrich

The Peabrain Politico Dictionary

Bipartisanship: Payouts to potential voters

Miranda warnings: Negotiating a
price with a hooker

Steering committee: The driving police

Where No Man Has Gone Before

If stupid politicians were playing roles in *Star Trek*, who would they be?

1. George Dubya Bush as Captain Jerk
2. John Kerry as Crock
3. Karl Rove as Commander Snot
4. Alberto Gonzales as Lieutenant Sue You
5. Duke Cunningham as Ensign Write-Off
6. Tom DeLay as Commander Rikers
7. Al Gore as Captain Discard
8. Donald Rumsfeld as Dr. Deploy
9. Marion Barry as Dr. Flusher
10. Ross Perot as Lieutenant Dwarf

Promises, Promises . . .

WHAT THE CANDIDATE PROMISES:
To increase housing opportunities and nutrition for the poor and underprivileged.

WHAT THE ELECTED OFFICIAL DOES:
Cuts tax breaks for Habitat for Humanity and closes every soup kitchen within fifty miles of his home.

Stupid Says . . .

66Politicians are like diapers. They both need changing regularly and for the same reason.99

—Author Unknown